Welcome

ALL THAT GLITTERS for the holiday season is just waiting for you inside *Country Woman Christmas 2011*. The latest book in our merry series for country-loving women, this Yuletide treasury is brimming with over 150 festive ideas to make your celebrations with family and friends as special as can be.

Just grab a cup of coffee, kick back and enjoy everything this cheery collection has to offer … from 110 scrumptious Christmas recipes and more than three dozen quick-and-easy craft projects to fun holiday theme parties and do-it-yourself decorations for the whole house.

You'll also find inspirational stories, heartwarming poetry and much more. Simply turn the page—and have a very merry Christmas!

16

Country Woman
Christmas
2011

74

ON THE COVER
Stocking Cake, p. 70

57

More Sparkle—All Year Long!
You don't have to wait until next Christmas to get more of the delightful recipes, crafts, decorations, stories and ideas featured in this book. They're in every issue of *Country Woman* magazine! To order for yourself or as a gift, visit *countrywomanmagazine.com* or call 1-888-861-1264.

Share Your Holiday Joy

DO YOU celebrate Christmas in a special way? If so, we'd like to know! We're already gathering material for the next edition of *Country Woman Christmas*. And we need your help!

Does your family carry on a unique holiday tradition? Or do you deck the halls in a creative way? Maybe you host a festive Christmas party or open house for friends and neighbors.

Do you have a nostalgic or inspirational story to share? Perhaps you've written holiday poetry or fiction.

We'd also like original Christmas craft projects and quilt patterns, plus handmade gifts, decorations, etc. And don't forget to include your best-loved recipes for holiday main courses, side dishes, appetizers, desserts, breads, cookies, candies, etc.

Send your ideas and/or photos to "CW Christmas Book," 5400 S. 60th St., Greendale WI 53129. (Enclose a self-addressed stamped envelope if you'd like your materials returned.) Or email your ideas and photos to *bookeditors@reimanpub.com* (write "CW Christmas" on the subject line).

©2011 Reiman Media Group, LLC
5400 S. 60th St., Greendale WI 53129
All rights reserved.

Taste of Home is a registered trademark of The Reader's Digest Association, Inc.

VICE PRESIDENT, EDITOR-IN-CHIEF: Catherine Cassidy

VICE PRESIDENT, EXECUTIVE EDITOR/BOOKS: Heidi Reuter Lloyd

CREATIVE DIRECTOR: Howard Greenberg

FOOD DIRECTOR: Diane Werner, RD

SENIOR EDITOR/BOOKS: Mark Hagen

EDITOR: Michelle Rozumalski

ASSOCIATE EDITORS: Amy Glander, Ellie Martin Cliffe

CRAFT EDITOR: Shalana Frisby

FOOD EDITOR: Wendy Stenman

ASSOCIATE CREATIVE DIRECTOR: Edwin Robles, Jr.

ART DIRECTOR: Rudy Krochalk

CONTENT PRODUCTION MANAGER: Julie Wagner

LAYOUT DESIGNER: Nancy Novak

COPY CHIEF: Deb Warlaumont Mulvey

PROOFREADER: Dulcie Shoener

RECIPE ASSET SYSTEM MANAGER: Coleen Martin

RECIPE TESTING AND EDITING: Taste of Home Test Kitchen

PHOTOGRAPHY: Taste of Home Photo Studio

ADMINISTRATIVE ASSISTANT: Barb Czysz

COVER PHOTO PHOTOGRAPHER: Rob Hagen

COVER FOOD STYLIST: Sarah Thompson

COVER SET STYLIST: Deone Jahnke

NORTH AMERICAN CHIEF MARKETING OFFICER: Lisa Karpinski

VICE PRESIDENT/BOOK MARKETING: Dan Fink

CREATIVE DIRECTOR/CREATIVE MARKETING: Jim Palmen

The Reader's Digest Association, Inc.

PRESIDENT AND CHIEF EXECUTIVE OFFICER: Tom Williams

EXECUTIVE VICE PRESIDENT, RDA, AND PRESIDENT, LIFESTYLE COMMUNITIES: Suzanne M. Grimes

International Standard Book Number: (10): 0-89821-870-5

International Standard Book Number: (13): 978-0-89821-870-1

International Standard Serial Number: 1093-6750

Timeless Recipes from Trusted Home Cooks® is a registered trademark of Reiman Media Group, Inc.

Printed in U.S.A.

For other Taste of Home books and products, visit *ShopTasteofHome.com*.

Christmas
DECORATING

Decking the halls with holiday cheer is as easy as can be when you rely on this do-it-yourself chapter.

Seat Feet

Large Christmas stockings make the perfect seasonal decorations for chairs around your kitchen or dining room table. Transform the shapes from flat to full by filling each stocking with a bit of polyester stuffing. To hang them on the backs of the chairs, just tie them on with ribbon.

Stockings Around the House

*Move beyond the fireplace mantel by dressing up every
room in your home with colorful socks for the holidays.*

HANGING over the hearth, Christmas stockings are a staple of the holiday season. But why limit these festive socks to just one spot? Take a step in a different direction with the fun-filled ideas here.

From a whimsical wreath to merry place markers, these around-the-house decorations will put your best foot forward for Christmas. (Turn to page 70 to bake our yummy Stocking Cake, too!)

Festive Foot Rests

Like to freshen up your furniture with accent pillows? You'll be head over heels for this idea! Our editors began with two purchased stockings featuring cuffs and pom-poms. After filling the stockings with polyester stuffing, they stitched underneath the cuff of each stocking to close the opening. Just fold the cuffs back down to conceal the stitches, then kick back and enjoy.

Well-Heeled Wreath

Christmas door decor doesn't get any simpler than this done-in-minutes accent. Hang any purchased decorative stocking in the center of a plain pine wreath, then accent the greenery with coordinating trims. In the photo at left, a strip of red fleece wrapped around the wreath and small white pom-poms glued on randomly mimic the snowman's scarf and hat.

Fun by the Foot

Who says bigger is better? Miniature stockings can make adorable trims in any nook, cranny or other small space. Here, felted wool socks with bold stripes are strung together on a coordinating cord for an instant room-brightener.

bright idea

To turn this garland into a decorative advent calendar, simply add a number to each stocking and tuck a small treat inside. Kids will get a real kick out of it!

Setting a Seasonal Pace

Personalize the place settings at your holiday table by topping them with monogrammed stockings featuring guests' initials. Or, add adhesive letters or fabric paint to stockings to spell out first names. These fun favors not only serve as place markers by revealing the seating arrangement, but also make perfect holders for napkins and flatware. If you like, stuff the stockings with special after-dinner treats such as wrapped Christmas cookies, chocolates or peppermint candies.

Stepping Up

These whimsical stockings hang from a metal basket holder—ideal for decorating a narrow corner in your home. (A coatrack or hat rack could work just as well.) To dress up the basket holder, our editors wrapped it with a bright ornament garland. Dangle any stockings you like, mixing different shapes and sizes for added interest.

Frosty Greenery

Transform a plain pine swag by embellishing it with shimmering white and silver ornaments, then add even more sparkle by wrapping it with coordinating lacy ribbons. Hanging along a fireplace mantel, the bedecked boughs will have a "fire and ice" effect against a blazing hearth or candlelight.

Dreaming of a
White Christmas

*Trimmed in wonderful white, your home will spread cheer
during the holiday season and all winter long.*

THE BEAUTY of a snow-covered landscape—it's an enduring image of Christmastime. Why not bring that winter wonder indoors? Decorate based on a delightfully white color palette using the ideas here.

Each understated accent is a snap to create, even during the hectic holiday season. Plus, you'll find all of the materials you need at craft stores, at discount stores or right in your own home.

Serving Up Snapshots

Why leave your favorite photos of outdoor winter fun in stashed-away albums? Display them in your home for all to enjoy. A white wood tray provides the perfect backdrop for snowy snapshots of loved ones. Our editors used a tray with an acrylic piece to cover their black-and-white photos. Wintry stickers accent the arrangement with splashes of color.

bright idea

The photo-filled tray above could also make a heartwarming gift for someone special on your list. For example, cover the bottom of the tray with pictures of grandkids to give to grandparents.

Snug in a Snowy Mug

Bring winter whimsy to your kitchen with an oversize ceramic mug (available in craft stores). The novelty cup can make a handy seasonal holder on the countertop for your spatulas, spoons and other tools. Plus, the plain mug is a cinch to dress up—just layer a white-dotted lime green ribbon over a coordinating ribbon and attach them to the center of the cup. It's that easy!

Draped Doilies

With their intricate patterns, white doilies resemble big, showy snowflakes. So why not add them to your decor? Our editors used a package of 6-inch doilies. Rather than peel the doilies apart into single pieces, they left several stuck together for each letter to create added stability. Then they put a silvery letter sticker in the center of each stack to spell "Peace" and threaded a narrow silver ribbon through the holes at the top.

Plates of Plenty

Plain white cake plates can make a lovely centerpiece topped with accents that fit a "white Christmas" theme. The wintry arrangement here showcases snow-tinged pinecones, frosty branches and ball ornaments atop stacked plates. You could also use snowflake tree ornaments or mini snowmen.

All Wrapped Up

Have an unused glass vase? Turn it into a luminary! Decorate a vellum sheet with a rub-on transfer and wrap the sheet around the outside of a clean vase. Then secure the ends in back using double-sided adhesive and add a candle. If the ends don't meet in back, attach a piece of ribbon to conceal the gap.

Christmas Luminaries

Let your days be merry and bright—create candlelit decorations that give your home a golden glow inside and out.

THE FLICKER of candlelight adds even more warmth and beauty to the holiday season. In this section, you'll learn how to make your own lovely luminaries for Christmastime.

With the vintage lantern, whimsical takeout containers, photo-trimmed vase and other illuminating but easy ideas here, you're sure to see December decorating in a whole new light.

Creativity With a Colander

Dotted with holes for draining, this everyday cooking tool makes a perfectly charming luminary for a country kitchen or dining table. Turn a silver or colored metal colander upside down and place a small battery-operated candle underneath to create pinpoints of golden light. On top, use the base of the inverted colander to hold an array of shimmering ball ornaments, pinecones or potpourri. Our editors completed the rustic centerpiece pictured above with a coordinating plaid ribbon tied in a bow.

bright idea

Want another fun option for the top of your colander luminary? Instead of finishing it off with an arrangement of ball ornaments, create an even brighter glow— use the inverted base for a votive candle or tea light in a holder.

Very Vintage Lantern

Give an ordinary hanging lantern a bit of antique appeal—you'll have a charming accent for the holiday season. To start, select scrapbook paper featuring a vintage Christmas pattern and photocopy it onto vellum paper using a black-and-white photocopier. Cut pieces of the vellum to fit behind each glass section of the lantern, secure the pieces in place and add a small battery-operated candle. Our editors embellished the handle on their creation with a flourish of red-and-green plaid ribbon for some cheery Christmas color.

Twinkling Takeout Containers

Sold in craft stores, colorful takeout containers can make cute luminaries in a flash. First, carefully remove the wire handle and unfold the container. Use a paper punch to punch stars in one or more sides, then reassemble the container and finish it off with a small battery-operated candle. This luminary is so fun and easy to create, you'll want to make a bunch!

Heartwarming Memories

The square glass vase below features built-in slots for inserting a picture (or photocopied picture) in each side. If you have a square glass vase without slots, simply photocopy your snapshots onto vellum paper, cut them to fit each side of the vase and attach them to the exterior. When your photos are in place, just insert a candle and enjoy.

Sweetly Sparkling

Old Christmas cookie cutters can become truly tasteful decorations when you try this easy holiday project. Apply clear tacky glue to the edge on one side of a large cookie cutter and place the glued edge down on a piece of lacy card stock. (Our editors used 4-1/2-inch and 5-inch cookie cutters and white card stock with a snowflake pattern.) When the glue is dry, carefully trim the excess card stock from around the edge of the cookie cutter. All that's left to do is stand it in front of a tea light or votive candle in a holder. How sweet it is!

From Green To Golden

Rustic containers switch from plants to candles thanks to the earthy idea here. These metal planters feature a decorative design around the top that allows golden light to shine through. Place these glowing accents outdoors along your walkway or on the porch.

Twelve Days of Christmas
Scavenger Hunt!

*Invite party guests to hunt around the house for 12 hidden objects,
then dig into a scrumptious themed meal.*

YOU'LL BE IN TUNE with the holiday season when you throw this fun-as-can-be December party. Inspired by the traditional carol, The Twelve Days of Christmas Scavenger Hunt is a festive event for young and old alike.

To host this merry get-together, simply gather 12 objects that represent the "gifts" described in the famous song. (See the lyrics of "The Twelve Days of Christmas" on page 23.)

For example, you could use a gold napkin ring to represent "five golden rings," a boot for "ten lords a-leaping," a child's toy recorder for "eleven pipers piping" or a white feather for "seven swans a-swimming."

On the day of your party, hide the objects around the house and give guests a scavenger hunt sheet listing the hidden items they'll be looking for. For each item, have a small wrapped prize for the person who finds it.

Don't forget the food! With a themed menu (see below) that includes delights such as Turkey Potpies, Turtle Dove Nests and Almond Pear Torte, your party will be in perfect harmony.

Party Menu

Cranberry Balsamic Salad	20
Turkey Potpies	20
Maids a-Milking Shakes . .	21
Deviled Eggs with Bacon .	21
Turtle Dove Nests	21
Almond Pear Torte	22
Winter Plum Punch	22

Cranberry Balsamic Salad

TOPPING:
1-1/2 cups all-purpose flour
    2 teaspoons sugar
1-1/2 teaspoons baking powder
    1 teaspoon dried thyme
  1/4 teaspoon baking soda
  1/4 teaspoon salt
    2 tablespoons cold butter
    1 cup buttermilk
    1 tablespoon canola oil

1. In a Dutch oven, saute mushrooms and onion in oil until tender. Stir in the turkey, peas and carrots, salt and pepper. Combine cornstarch and broth until smooth; gradually stir into the pan. Bring to a boil. Reduce heat; cook and stir for 2 minutes or until thickened. Stir in sour cream. Transfer to eight greased 8-oz. ramekins.

2. In a large bowl, combine the flour, sugar, baking powder, thyme, baking soda and salt. Cut in butter until the mixture resembles coarse crumbs. In a small bowl, combine buttermilk and oil; stir into dry ingredients just until moistened. Drop by heaping teaspoonfuls over filling.

3. Bake, uncovered, at 400° for 20-25 minutes or until topping is golden brown and filling is bubbly. Let stand 10 minutes before serving. **Yield:** 8 servings.

Cranberry Balsamic Salad

—*Patricia Slater, Pefferlaw, Ontario*

    3 cups fresh baby spinach
    3 cups torn mixed salad greens
    2 medium navel oranges, sectioned
  1/3 cup crumbled feta cheese
  1/4 cup chopped red onion
  1/2 cup balsamic vinaigrette
    2 tablespoons orange juice
    1 teaspoon grated orange peel
  1/2 cup dried cranberries
    2 tablespoons sliced almonds, toasted

In a large bowl, combine the spinach, salad greens, oranges, cheese and red onion. In a small bowl, whisk the vinaigrette, orange juice and peel. Drizzle over salad; toss to coat. Sprinkle with cranberries and almonds. **Yield:** 8 servings.

Turkey Potpies

—*Lily Julow, Gainesville, Florida*

4-1/3 cups sliced baby portobello mushrooms
    1 large onion, chopped
    1 tablespoon olive oil
2-1/2 cups cubed cooked turkey
    1 package (16 ounces) frozen peas and carrots
  1/4 teaspoon salt
  1/4 teaspoon pepper
  1/4 cup cornstarch
2-1/2 cups chicken broth
  1/4 cup sour cream

Turkey Potpies

Maids a-Milking Shakes

—Taste of Home Test Kitchen

1-1/2 cups 2% milk
4-1/2 cups vanilla ice cream
   15 mint creme Oreo cookies, crushed
  1/2 teaspoon peppermint extract
Whipped cream and additional crushed mint creme Oreo
  cookies

In a blender, combine milk, ice cream, cookies and extract;
cover and process until smooth. Pour into chilled glasses.
Garnish with whipped cream and additional cookies. Serve
immediately. **Yield: 5 servings.**

Maids a-Milking Shakes

Deviled Eggs with Bacon

—Barbara Reid, Mounds, Oklahoma

  12 hard-cooked eggs
 1/3 cup mayonnaise
   3 bacon strips, cooked and crumbled
   3 tablespoons finely chopped red onion
   3 tablespoons sweet pickle relish
 1/4 teaspoon smoked paprika

Cut eggs in half lengthwise. Remove yolks; set whites aside. In
a small bowl, mash yolks. Add the mayonnaise, bacon, onion
and relish; mix well. Stuff into egg whites. Refrigerate until
serving. Sprinkle with paprika. **Yield: 2 dozen.**

Turtle Dove Nests

Turtle Dove Nests

—Taste of Home Test Kitchen

    1 package (11 ounces) peanut butter and milk
      chocolate chips
2-1/2 cups crispy rice noodles
 1/3 cup crisp rice cereal
 1/3 cup chopped salted peanuts
  45 blue jelly beans

1. In a microwave, melt chips; stir until smooth. Stir in the
rice noodles, cereal and peanuts.

2. Divide mixture into 15 mounds on a waxed paper-lined
baking sheet. Using fingers, shape each into a nest; press an
indentation in the center of nest. Fill each nest with three
jelly beans. Let stand until set. Store in an airtight container.
Yield: 15 servings.

Deviled Eggs with Bacon

Winter Plum Punch
—*Taste of Home Test Kitchen*

     5 cups water, *divided*
Assorted fresh fruit (cranberries and lemon and orange slices)
Fresh mint leaves
Cinnamon sticks (3 inches), crushed
     1 cup plum jam
     1 teaspoon ground cinnamon
    1/2 teaspoon ground nutmeg
     4 cups cranberry juice, chilled
     1 cup orange juice, chilled
    1/4 cup lemon juice
     4 cups club soda, chilled

1. Lightly coat a decorative tube cake pan or gelatin mold with cooking spray; add 1/2 cup of water. Arrange fruit, mint and cinnamon pieces in pan as desired. Freeze until solid. Add remaining water; arrange more fruit, mint and cinnamon pieces as desired. Freeze until ready to use.

2. In a microwave, melt the plum jam; stir until smooth. Add cinnamon and nutmeg. Cool. Just before serving, in a punch bowl, combine the juices and plum mixture. Stir in soda.

3. Unmold ice ring by wrapping the bottom of the mold in a hot, damp dishcloth. Invert onto a baking sheet; place fruit side up in punch bowl. **Yield:** 13 servings (3/4 cup each).

Almond Pear Torte

Almond Pear Torte
—*Trisha Kruse, Eagle, Idaho*

1-1/3 cups all-purpose flour
  3/4 cup butter, softened
  1/2 cup sugar
  1/2 cup ground almonds, toasted
  1/4 teaspoon ground nutmeg
FILLING:
    2 packages (8 ounces *each*) cream cheese, softened
  1/4 cup packed brown sugar
  1/4 teaspoon almond extract
    2 eggs
TOPPING:
  1/2 cup packed brown sugar
  1/4 teaspoon ground nutmeg
    3 cups thinly sliced peeled fresh pears
  1/2 cup slivered almonds

1. In a small bowl, combine flour, butter, sugar, almonds and nutmeg. Press onto the bottom of a greased 9-in. springform pan; set aside.

2. In a large bowl, beat the cream cheese, brown sugar and extract until smooth. Add the eggs; beat on low speed just until combined. Pour over crust. For topping, combine brown sugar and nutmeg. Add pears; toss to coat. Arrange over top. Sprinkle with almonds.

3. Bake at 350° for 50-60 minutes or until center is almost set. Cool on a wire rack for 10 minutes. Carefully run a knife around edge of pan to loosen; cool 1 hour longer. Refrigerate leftovers. **Yield:** 14 servings.

Winter Plum Punch

❋ *Special Feature* ❋

The Twelve Days of Christmas

On the 1st day of Christmas
My true love sent to me
A partridge in a pear tree.

On the 2nd day of Christmas
My true love sent to me
Two turtle doves
And a partridge in a pear tree.

On the 3rd day of Christmas
My true love sent to me
Three French hens
Two turtle doves
And a partridge in a pear tree.

On the 4th day of Christmas
My true love sent to me
Four calling birds
Three French hens
Two turtle doves
And a partridge in a pear tree.

On the 5th day of Christmas
My true love sent to me
Five golden rings
Four calling birds
Three French hens
Two turtle doves
And a partridge in a pear tree.

On the 6th day of Christmas
My true love sent to me
Six geese a-laying
Five golden rings
Four calling birds
Three French hens
Two turtle doves
And a partridge in a pear tree.

On the 7th day of Christmas
My true love sent to me
Seven swans a-swimming
Six geese a-laying
Five golden rings
Four calling birds
Three French hens
Two turtle doves
And a partridge in a pear tree.

On the 8th day of Christmas
My true love sent to me
Eight maids a-milking
Seven swans a-swimming
Six geese a-laying
Five golden rings
Four calling birds
Three French hens
Two turtle doves
And a partridge in a pear tree.

On the 9th day of Christmas
My true love sent to me
Nine ladies dancing
Eight maids a-milking
Seven swans a-swimming
Six geese a-laying
Five golden rings
Four calling birds
Three French hens
Two turtle doves
And a partridge in a pear tree.

On the 10th day of Christmas
My true love sent to me
Ten lords a-leaping
Nine ladies dancing
Eight maids a-milking
Seven swans a-swimming
Six geese a-laying
Five golden rings
Four calling birds
Three French hens
Two turtle doves
And a partridge in a pear tree.

On the 11th day of Christmas
My true love sent to me
Eleven pipers piping
Ten lords a-leaping
Nine ladies dancing
Eight maids a-milking
Seven swans a-swimming
Six geese a-laying
Five golden rings
Four calling birds
Three French hens
Two turtle doves
And a partridge in a pear tree.

On the 12th day of Christmas
My true love sent to me
Twelve drummers drumming
Eleven pipers piping
Ten lords a-leaping
Nine ladies dancing
Eight maids a-milking
Seven swans a-swimming
Six geese a-laying
Five golden rings
Four calling birds
Three French hens
Two turtle doves
And a partridge in a pear tree!

Holiday
RECIPES

Make the season scrumptious with this chapter of elegant appetizers, savory main courses, decadent desserts and more.

Citrus-Raspberry Coffee Cake

On Christmas morning, warm hearts by serving Sausage Cranberry Pancakes, Apple Fritters, Mushroom-Spinach Bake or any of the sunrise specialties here.

Citrus-Raspberry Coffee Cake

Orange and lemon nicely complement the berries in this dense cake. I like to dress it up with a dusting of confectioners' sugar.
—Pat Harlow, Cataldo, Idaho

   3 cups all-purpose flour
   2 cups sugar
   3 teaspoons baking powder
   1 teaspoon salt
   4 eggs
   1 cup canola oil
1/2 cup orange juice
   1 teaspoon lemon extract
   2 cups fresh *or* frozen unsweetened raspberries
Confectioners' sugar

1. In a large bowl, combine the flour, sugar, baking powder and salt. In another bowl, combine the eggs, oil, orange juice and extract. Stir into dry ingredients just until moistened.

2. Pour half of the batter into a greased and floured 10-in. fluted tube pan. Sprinkle with berries. Top with remaining batter. Bake at 350° for 55-65 minutes or until a toothpick inserted near the center comes out clean.

3. Cool in pan for 10 minutes before removing from pan to a wire rack to cool completely. Dust with confectioners' sugar. **Yield:** 16 servings.

Editor's Note: If using frozen raspberries, do not thaw before adding to batter.

Artichoke & Spinach Eggs Benedict

This rich, creamy classic starring fresh artichokes is sure to make your guests feel indulged. —Lori Wiese, Humboldt, Minnesota

   1 envelope hollandaise sauce mix
   4 medium artichokes
   4 eggs
   1 tablespoon chopped green onion
   2 tablespoons butter
   2 tablespoons all-purpose flour
   1 cup half-and-half cream
   1 package (10 ounces) frozen chopped spinach,
     thawed and squeezed dry
   2 teaspoons lemon juice
1/8 teaspoon salt
1/8 teaspoon pepper
   3 tablespoons shredded Parmesan cheese
Paprika

1. Prepare sauce mix according to package directions. Set aside and keep warm.

2. Using a sharp knife, cut stems from artichokes. Remove and discard outer leaves, leaving each artichoke bottom exposed. Cut off tops 1/2 in. above the artichoke bottoms and discard. With a grapefruit spoon, carefully remove the fuzzy centers and discard. Place artichoke bottoms in a large saucepan; add 1 in. of water. Bring to a boil. Reduce heat; cover and simmer for 15-20 minutes or until tender.

3. Place 2-3 in. of water in a large skillet with high sides. Bring to a boil; reduce heat and simmer gently. Break cold eggs, one at a time, into a custard cup or saucer. Holding the cup close to the surface of the water, slip each egg into water. Cook, uncovered, until whites are completely set and yolks are still soft, about 4 minutes.

4. Meanwhile, in a large skillet, saute green onion in butter until tender. Stir in flour until blended; gradually add cream. Bring to a boil; cook and stir for 1-2 minutes or until thickened. Add the spinach, lemon juice, salt and pepper; heat through. Remove from the heat; stir in cheese until melted.

5. With a slotted spoon, lift each egg out of the water. On each artichoke bottom, place 1/3 cup spinach mixture, a poached egg and 1/3 cup hollandaise sauce. Sprinkle with paprika. Serve immediately. **Yield:** 4 servings.

Artichoke & Spinach Eggs Benedict

Mushroom-Spinach Bake

With a yummy filling and golden-brown topping of cheese, this souffle-like egg dish is a holiday staple at our house.
—Frederick Hilliard, Charleston, West Virginia

      3 tablespoons plus 1-1/2 teaspoons butter
  1/2 cup all-purpose flour
      2 cups 2% milk
      4 eggs, lightly beaten
      1 cup (4 ounces) shredded Gruyere *or* Swiss cheese
  1/2 teaspoon salt
  1/8 teaspoon pepper
Dash ground nutmeg
MUSHROOM SPINACH FILLING:
      2 cups sliced baby portobello mushrooms
      1 tablespoon chopped shallot
      1 tablespoon butter
      1 teaspoon white truffle oil, optional
      1 package (10 ounces) frozen chopped spinach,
         thawed and squeezed dry
      1 tablespoon all-purpose flour
  1/8 teaspoon salt
  1/8 teaspoon pepper
  1/4 cup heavy whipping cream
  1/3 cup shredded Gruyere *or* Swiss cheese

1. In a large saucepan, melt the butter. Stir in the flour until smooth; gradually add milk. Bring to a boil; cook and stir for 1-2 minutes or until thickened.

2. Stir a small amount of hot mixture into eggs. Return all to the pan, stirring constantly. Stir in the cheese, salt, pepper and nutmeg; set aside.

3. For filling, in a large skillet, saute mushrooms and shallot in butter and oil if desired until tender. Add spinach; cook

Mushroom-Spinach Bake

1 minute longer. Stir in flour, salt and pepper until blended. Gradually add cream; heat through (do not boil).

4. Pour half of egg mixture into a greased 8-in. square baking dish. Top with filling and remaining egg mixture. Sprinkle with cheese. Bake at 400° for 20-25 minutes or until a knife inserted near the center comes out clean. **Yield: 6 servings.**

Strawberry French Toast Bake

The owners of the Morley House Bed & Breakfast in Gatlinburg, Tennessee, shared this special recipe with me. It's so good!
—Valerie Mitchell, Olathe, Kansas

      1 package (8 ounces) cream cheese, softened
     16 slices bread, crusts removed
     10 eggs
  1-1/2 cups half-and-half cream
  1/2 cup butter, melted
  1/4 cup maple syrup
STRAWBERRY SAUCE:
      1 jar (18 ounces) strawberry preserves
      2 cups sliced fresh strawberries

1. Spread cream cheese over eight slices of bread; top with remaining bread. Cut sandwiches into 1-in. squares; place in a greased 13-in. x 9-in. baking dish. In a small bowl, combine the eggs, cream, butter and syrup; pour into the dish. With a spoon, gently press bread cubes into egg mixture. Cover and refrigerate for 8 hours or overnight.

2. Remove from refrigerator 30 minutes before baking. Bake at 350° for 35-40 minutes or until a knife inserted near the center comes out clean and top is golden brown. Let stand for 10 minutes before serving.

3. For the sauce, in a small saucepan, combine preserves and strawberries. Cook and stir until preserves are melted. Serve with French toast bake. **Yield: 8 servings (2-1/2 cups sauce).**

Spiced Apricot Tea

A chilly winter's morning is no match for a steaming cup of this fruity tea spiced with cinnamon sticks and cloves.
—Mary Houchin, Lebanon, Illinois

      2 cinnamon sticks (3 inches)
     10 whole cloves
      3 cups water
      2 individual tea bags
      3 cups apricot nectar
  2/3 cup sugar
  1/4 cup lemon juice

1. Place the cinnamon and cloves on a double thickness of cheesecloth; bring up corners of cloth and tie with string to form a bag.

2. Place water in a large saucepan. Bring to a boil. Remove from the heat. Add tea bags and spice bag; cover and steep for 5 minutes. Discard tea bags and spice bag. Stir in nectar, sugar and juice; heat through. Serve warm. **Yield: 6 servings.**

Savory Breakfast Muffins

These hearty muffins loaded with cheese, ham, sweet red pepper and green onions are a great accompaniment to eggs.
—Michelle Van Maanen, Lethbridge, Alberta

1-1/2 cups whole wheat flour
   1/2 cup all-purpose flour
     2 teaspoons baking powder
   1/2 teaspoon baking soda
   1/2 teaspoon salt
   1/2 teaspoon pepper
     2 eggs
1-1/4 cups buttermilk
     2 tablespoons butter, melted
     1 tablespoon canola oil
   3/4 cup cubed Havarti cheese with jalapeno *or*
      pepper Jack cheese
   3/4 cup finely chopped fully cooked ham
     1 medium sweet red pepper, finely chopped
     4 green onions, finely chopped

1. In a large bowl, combine flours, baking powder, baking soda, salt and pepper. In another bowl, combine the eggs, buttermilk, butter and oil. Stir into dry ingredients just until moistened. Fold in remaining ingredients.

2. Fill greased or paper-lined muffin cups three-fourths full. Bake at 400° for 18-22 minutes or until a toothpick inserted in muffin comes out clean. Cool for 5 minutes before removing from pans to wire racks. Serve warm. **Yield:** 16 muffins.

Berry Waldorf Salad

Everyone in my family loves this tangy fruit medley. Pecans and celery add crunch while a creamy dressing brings it all together.
—Carolyn Johns, Lacey, Washington

1-1/4 cups (10 ounces) vanilla yogurt
     2 tablespoons sugar
   1/8 teaspoon ground cardamom
     2 cups fresh *or* frozen raspberries
   1/2 cup fresh *or* frozen blackberries
     1 cup fresh cranberries
     1 celery rib, chopped
   1/2 cup golden raisins
   1/4 cup chopped pecans

In a small bowl, whisk the yogurt, sugar and cardamom. In a large bowl, combine the berries, celery and raisins; add yogurt mixture and toss to coat. Cover and refrigerate for 1 hour. Just before serving, sprinkle with pecans. **Yield:** 6 servings.

Sausage Cranberry Pancakes

Why serve plain pancakes for Christmas? These fluffy flapjacks burst with orange, sausage and cranberry flavor in every bite.
—Debbie Reid, Clearwater, Florida

     1 pound bulk pork sausage
   1/3 cup dried cranberries
   1/3 cup orange juice
1-1/2 cups all-purpose flour

Sausage Cranberry Pancakes

     3 tablespoons baking powder
   1/4 teaspoon salt
     1 egg
1-1/2 cups 2% milk
     3 tablespoons maple syrup
     1 tablespoon canola oil
     2 teaspoons grated orange peel
Additional maple syrup

1. In a large skillet, cook sausage over medium heat until no longer pink; drain.

2. Meanwhile, place cranberries in a small bowl. Cover with orange juice; let stand for 5 minutes.

3. Drain cranberries, reserving the juice. In a large bowl, combine the flour, baking powder and salt. In another bowl, whisk the egg, milk, maple syrup, oil and orange peel; add to dry ingredients just until moistened. Stir in cranberries, sausage and reserved juice.

4. Pour the batter by 1/4 cupfuls onto a greased hot griddle; turn when bubbles form on top. Cook until the second side is golden brown. Serve with syrup. **Yield:** 24 pancakes.

Cran-Blueberry Smoothies

A honey-sweetened blend of three fruits, vanilla yogurt and milk, this pretty purple beverage is a thirst-quenching delight.
—Lisa Lindsay, Baton Rouge, Louisiana

     1 cup frozen cranberries
     1 cup fresh *or* frozen unsweetened blueberries
     1 medium banana, cut up
   1/2 cup 2% milk
   1/2 cup vanilla yogurt
     1 tablespoon honey

Place all ingredients in a blender; cover and process until smooth. Pour into chilled glasses; serve immediately. **Yield:** 3 servings.

Apple Fritters

Apple Fritters

I've been frying these for more than 25 years because my family can't get enough of them. I'm thankful they're easy to make!
—*Mary Shivers, Ada, Oklahoma*

        3 cups all-purpose flour
    1/2 cup sugar
        2 teaspoons baking powder
    1/2 teaspoon salt
        1 egg, beaten
        1 cup milk
    1/4 cup orange juice
    1/4 cup butter, melted
        1 teaspoon vanilla extract
        1 teaspoon grated orange peel
        1 cup grated unpeeled apples
Oil for deep-fat frying
Confectioners' sugar

1. In a large bowl, combine the flour, sugar, baking powder and salt. Combine the egg, milk, orange juice, butter, vanilla and orange peel; add to dry ingredients just until moistened. Fold in the apples.

2. In an electric skillet or deep fryer, heat oil to 375°. Drop batter by rounded tablespoonfuls, a few at a time, into hot oil. Fry until golden brown, about 1-2 minutes on each side. Drain on paper towels. Dust with confectioners' sugar. **Yield:** about 3-1/2 dozen.

Ratatouille Quiche

This cheesy quiche features a bounty of vegetables. We love the rich flavors that develop when the veggies caramelize.
—*Lily Julow, Gainesville, Florida*

Pastry for single-crust pie (9 inches)
        1 small eggplant, peeled
        1 medium zucchini
        1 medium green pepper
        1 medium tomato, seeded
        1 small onion
        2 tablespoons olive oil
        1 garlic clove, minced
        1 cup (4 ounces) shredded Swiss cheese
        6 eggs
        2 cups half-and-half cream
    1/2 teaspoon salt
    1/4 teaspoon pepper

1. Unroll pastry into a 9-in. deep-dish pie plate; flute edges. Line unpricked pastry with a double thickness of heavy-duty foil. Bake at 450° for 8 minutes. Remove foil; bake 5 minutes longer. Cool on a wire rack.

2. Finely chop the eggplant, zucchini, green pepper, tomato and onion. In a large skillet, saute vegetables in oil until tender. Add garlic; cook 1 minute longer. Transfer to prepared pastry; sprinkle with cheese.

3. In a large bowl, whisk the eggs, cream, salt and pepper; pour over cheese. Bake at 350° for 40-45 minutes or until a knife inserted near the center comes out clean. Let stand for 10 minutes before serving. **Yield:** 6 servings.

Breakfast Enchiladas

Smothered with melted cheese and sauce, this Southwestern dish is always popular. Chorizo sausage gives it a nice kick.
—*Tahnia Fox, Trenton, Michigan*

    1/2 pound uncooked chorizo *or* spicy pork sausage
        1 small onion, finely chopped
    1/2 medium green pepper, finely chopped
        2 teaspoons butter
        6 eggs, beaten
    3/4 cup shredded cheddar cheese, *divided*
    3/4 cup shredded pepper Jack cheese, *divided*
        2 cans (10 ounces *each*) enchilada sauce, *divided*
        8 flour tortillas (8 inches), room temperature
        1 green onion, finely chopped

1. Crumble chorizo into a large skillet; add onion and green pepper. Cook over medium heat for 6-8 minutes or until the sausage is fully cooked; drain.

2. In another skillet, heat butter over medium heat. Add eggs; cook and stir until almost set. Remove from the heat; stir in the chorizo mixture and 1/3 cup of each cheese.

3. Spread 1/2 cup enchilada sauce into a greased 13-in. x 9-in. baking dish. Spread 2 tablespoons enchilada sauce over each tortilla; place 2 tablespoons egg mixture down the center. Roll up and place seam side down in prepared dish.

4. Pour remaining enchilada sauce over the top; sprinkle with remaining cheeses.

5. Bake, uncovered, at 350° for 25-30 minutes or until heated through. Sprinkle with green onion. **Yield:** 8 servings.

Breakfast Enchiladas

Classic Fruit Kolaches

Bountiful Breads

From golden-brown loaves and sweet coffee cakes to fruit-filled muffins and tender rolls, the bakery-worthy favorites featured here are sure to spread cheer.

Classic Fruit Kolaches

We love making these melt-in-your-mouth goodies. For extra fun, use Christmas cookie cutters instead of a biscuit cutter.
—Glen & Sue Ellen Borkholder, Sturgis, Michigan

    6 to 7 cups all-purpose flour
  1/4 cup sugar
    2 packages (1/4 ounce *each*) active dry yeast
    2 teaspoons salt
    2 cups 2% milk
  1/2 cup butter, cubed
  1/2 cup water
    6 egg yolks
  1/4 cup butter, melted
    1 can (12 ounces) raspberry *and/or* apricot cake and
      pastry filling
ICING:
    3 cups confectioners' sugar
  1/4 cup butter, softened
    2 teaspoons vanilla extract
  1/2 teaspoon salt
    4 to 6 tablespoons 2% milk

1. In a large bowl, combine 3 cups flour, sugar, yeast and salt. In a large saucepan, heat the milk, cubed butter and water to 120°-130°. Add to dry ingredients; beat just until moistened. Add egg yolks; beat until smooth. Stir in enough remaining flour to form a soft dough (dough will be sticky). Do not knead. Cover and let rise until doubled, about 45 minutes.

2. Turn dough onto a floured surface; roll to 1/2-in. thickness. Cut with a floured 2-1/2-in. biscuit cutter. Place 2 in. apart on lightly greased baking sheets. Brush with melted butter. Cover; let rise in a warm place until doubled, about 30 minutes.

3. Using the back of a spoon, make an indentation in the center of each roll. Spoon a heaping teaspoonful of raspberry or apricot filling into each indentation. Bake at 350° for 15-20 minutes or until golden brown. Remove from pans to wire racks to cool.

4. Combine the confectioners' sugar, butter, vanilla, salt and enough milk to achieve desired consistency. Drizzle over rolls. **Yield:** 2-1/2 dozen.

Editor's Note: This recipe was tested with Solo brand cake and pastry filling. Look for it in the baking aisle.

Rye Onion Bread

A warm loaf of this earthy bread is a wonderful accompaniment to soups and stews.   *—Carol Fegley, Lavelle, Pennsylvania*

    Cornmeal
    2 to 2-3/4 cups all-purpose flour
 1-1/2 cups rye flour
  1/2 cup finely chopped onion
    3 tablespoons sugar
    2 tablespoons caraway seeds
    1 teaspoon salt
    1 package (1/4 ounce) active dry yeast
 1-1/2 cups 2% milk
    3 tablespoons butter
    1 egg white
 1-1/2 teaspoons water

1. Grease a 9-in. x 5-in. loaf pan and sprinkle lightly with cornmeal; set aside.

2. In a large bowl, combine 1 cup all-purpose flour, rye flour, onion, sugar, caraway, salt and yeast. In a small saucepan, heat the milk and butter to 120°-130°. Add to dry ingredients; beat just until moistened. Stir in enough remaining all-purpose flour to form a firm dough.

3. Turn dough onto a floured surface; knead until smooth and elastic, about 6-8 minutes. Place in a greased bowl, turning once to grease the top. Cover and let rise in a warm place until doubled, about 1 hour.

4. Punch dough down. Shape into a loaf. Place in prepared pan. Cover and let rise until doubled, about 30 minutes. Combine egg white and water; brush over loaf. Bake at 350° for 40-45 minutes or until golden brown. Remove from pan to a wire rack to cool completely. **Yield:** 1 loaf (16 slices).

Rye Onion Bread

Khachapuri

While in Russia, where we adopted our two children, my husband and I discovered these tasty little rounds filled with cheese.
—Rachel Sauder, Tremont, Illinois

    3-1/2 teaspoons active dry yeast
      3/4 cup warm milk (110° to 115°)
        6 tablespoons butter, melted
        2 tablespoons honey
        2 to 2-1/2 cups all-purpose flour
        1 teaspoon salt
      1/4 teaspoon ground coriander
    FILLING:
        1 egg, lightly beaten
      12 ounces brick cheese, shredded

1. In a large bowl, dissolve yeast in warm milk. Stir in butter and honey. In another bowl, combine 1-3/4 cups flour, salt and coriander; gradually add to yeast mixture, beating until smooth. Stir in enough remaining flour to form a soft dough.

2. Turn onto a lightly floured surface; knead until smooth and elastic, about 6-8 minutes. Place in a greased bowl, turning once to grease top. Cover and let rise in a warm place until doubled, about 1 hour.

3. Punch the dough down. Let rise until doubled, about 30 minutes. Turn onto a lightly floured surface; divide into six balls. Roll each into 6-1/2-in. circles.

4. In a small bowl, combine the egg and cheese. Mound about 1/2 cup cheese mixture in the center of each circle. Fold the dough over filling, gathering and twisting into a knot to seal. Place on an ungreased baking sheet. Let stand for 10 minutes. Bake at 375° for 30-35 minutes or until lightly browned. Serve immediately. **Yield:** 6 servings.

Khachapuri

Savory Surprise Buns

These golden bites are always a holiday hit. The creamy, garlicky center perfectly complements the bread surrounding it.
—Elizabeth Prestie, Preeceville, Saskatchewan

    3-3/4 to 4-1/4 cups all-purpose flour
      1/4 cup sugar
        1 tablespoon quick-rise yeast
      1/2 teaspoon salt
    1-1/2 cups water
        3 tablespoons canola oil
        1 egg
        1 cup garlic-herb cheese spread
        1 tablespoon butter, melted

1. In a large bowl, combine 2-1/2 cups flour, sugar, yeast and salt. In a small saucepan, heat water and oil to 120°-130°. Add to dry ingredients; beat just until moistened. Add egg; beat until smooth. Stir in enough remaining flour to form a soft dough (dough will be sticky).

2. Turn onto a floured surface; knead until smooth and elastic, about 6-8 minutes. Place in a greased bowl, turning once to grease top. Cover and let rise in a warm place until doubled, about 30 minutes.

3. Punch dough down. Turn onto a floured surface; divide into four portions. Roll each portion into a 9-in. x 6-in. rectangle. Cut into 3-in. squares.

4. Place 2 teaspoons cheese spread in center of each square. Moisten corners with water; bring over center of filling and pinch corners tightly in center. Place seam side down on greased baking sheets.

5. Bake at 350° for 12-15 minutes or until golden brown. Brush tops with butter. **Yield:** 2 dozen.

Stollen for a Crowd

Expecting lots of guests? Consider this versatile stollen. You can bake it in advance and freeze it. Later, when the pastry is thawed, simply sprinkle on confectioners' sugar and serve.
—Ruth Hartunian Alumbaugh, Willimantic, Connecticut

    4-1/2 to 5-1/2 cups all-purpose flour
        1 package (9 ounces) yellow cake mix
        2 packages (1/4 ounce *each*) active dry yeast
      1/4 teaspoon salt
    2-1/2 cups warm water (120° to 130°)
        2 cans (12-1/2 ounces *each*) poppy seed cake and
          pastry filling
        1 tablespoon confectioners' sugar

1. In a large bowl, combine 3 cups flour, cake mix, yeast and salt. Add water to dry ingredients; beat just until moistened. Stir in enough remaining flour to form a soft dough (dough will be sticky).

2. Turn onto a floured surface; knead until smooth and elastic, about 6-8 minutes. Place in a very large greased bowl, turning once to grease the top. Cover and let rise in a warm place until doubled, about 1 hour.

3. Punch dough down; turn onto a floured surface. Divide in half. Roll each half into a 12-in. x 8-in. oval. Spread each with 1 can filling. Fold a long side over to within 1 in. of opposite side; press edges lightly to seal. Place on greased baking sheets. Cover and let rise until doubled, about 30 minutes.

4. Bake at 350° for 25-30 minutes or until golden brown. Remove to wire racks to cool. Sprinkle with confectioners' sugar. **Yield:** 2 loaves (16 slices each).

Editor's Note: This recipe was tested with Solo brand cake and pastry filling. Look for it in the baking aisle.

Golden Honey Rolls

These yummy, honey-sweetened rolls are popular at our family gatherings. Once, upon seeing the pan was empty, a disappointed relative asked me, "Could you make more next year?"
—*Ellen Krueger, Canton, Missouri*

Sun-Dried Tomato Focaccia

      1 package (1/4 ounce) active dry yeast
      1 cup warm 2% milk (110° to 115°)
   1/2 cup canola oil
      2 tablespoons honey
      1 egg
      1 egg yolk
      1 teaspoon salt
 3-1/4 to 3-3/4 cups all-purpose flour
TOPPING:
   1/3 cup confectioners' sugar
      2 tablespoons butter, softened
      1 tablespoon honey
      1 egg white

1. In a large bowl, dissolve yeast in warm milk. Add the oil, honey, egg, egg yolk, salt and 2 cups flour. Beat on medium speed for 3 minutes. Stir in enough remaining flour to form a soft dough. Dough will be sticky.

2. Turn dough onto a floured surface; knead until smooth and elastic, about 6-8 minutes. Place in a greased bowl, turning once to grease the top. Cover and let rise in a warm place until doubled, about 1 hour. Punch dough down. Divide into 20 pieces. Shape each into a ball. Divide between two greased 9-in. round baking pans. Combine the topping ingredients; brush 3 tablespoons over the rolls. Cover and let rise until doubled, about 30 minutes. Brush with remaining topping.

3. Bake at 350° for 18-20 minutes or until golden brown. Remove from pans to wire racks. **Yield:** 20 rolls.

Sun-Dried Tomato Focaccia

Take advantage of your bread machine to make this savory loaf. With tomatoes and onions on top, it tastes as good as it looks.
—*Kathy Katz, Ocala, Florida*

   1/4 cup chopped sun-dried tomatoes (not packed in oil)
   1/2 cup boiling water
 1-1/4 cups warm V8 juice (70° to 80°)
      2 tablespoons olive oil
   1/4 cup grated Parmesan cheese
      1 tablespoon dried parsley flakes
      2 teaspoons sugar
      1 teaspoon salt
      1 teaspoon dried basil
   1/2 teaspoon garlic powder
      2 cups whole wheat flour
 1-1/2 cups all-purpose flour
      2 teaspoons active dry yeast
TOPPING:
      2 tablespoons slivered sun-dried tomatoes
         (not packed in oil)
   1/4 cup boiling water
     12 thin slices red onion, halved
      1 tablespoon olive oil

1. In a small bowl, combine chopped sun-dried tomatoes and boiling water. Let stand for 5 minutes; drain.

2. In bread machine pan, place warm V8 juice, oil, softened tomatoes, cheese, parsley, sugar, salt, basil, garlic powder, flours and yeast in order suggested by manufacturer. Select the dough setting (check dough after 5 minutes of mixing; add 1 to 2 tablespoons of water or flour if needed).

3. In a small bowl, combine slivered sun-dried tomatoes and boiling water. Let stand for 5 minutes; drain and pat dry with paper towels.

4. When the bread machine cycle is completed, turn the dough onto a lightly floured surface. Punch dough down. Divide in half; roll each portion into a 9-in. circle. Transfer to two greased 9-in. round baking pans.

5. Using the end of a wooden spoon handle, make 1/4-in. indentations in dough. Arrange tomato slivers and onion slices over dough; press down lightly. Cover and let rise in a warm place until doubled, about 30 minutes. Brush with oil. Bake at 375° for 20-25 minutes or until golden brown. Remove to wire racks. **Yield:** 2 loaves (8 servings each).

Glazed Coconut-Banana Bread

Glazed Coconut-Banana Bread

Give your Christmas celebration a refreshing taste of the tropics with this yummy variation of banana bread. It's quick to prepare, leaving you plenty of time to focus on other holiday details.
—Katherine Nelson, Centerville, Utah

    1/4 cup butter, softened
      1 cup sugar
      2 eggs
1-1/2 cups mashed ripe bananas (2 to 3 medium)
    1/4 cup reduced-fat plain yogurt
      3 tablespoons unsweetened apple juice
    1/2 teaspoon vanilla extract
      2 cups all-purpose flour
    3/4 teaspoon baking soda
    1/2 teaspoon salt
    1/2 cup plus 1 tablespoon flaked coconut, *divided*
    1/2 cup confectioners' sugar
      1 tablespoon lime juice

1. In a large bowl, cream butter and sugar until crumbly. Add eggs, one at a time, beating well after each addition. Stir in the bananas, yogurt, apple juice and vanilla. Combine the flour, baking soda and salt; add to creamed mixture. Stir in 1/2 cup coconut.

2. Transfer to a greased 9-in. x 5-in. loaf pan. Sprinkle with remaining coconut. Bake at 350° for 50-55 minutes or until a toothpick inserted near the center comes out clean. Cool for 10 minutes before removing from pan to a wire rack.

3. Combine confectioners' sugar and lime juice; drizzle over warm bread. **Yield:** 1 loaf (16 slices).

Almond Danish Coffee Cakes

With one bite, your family will know these were a labor of love. Sweet almond paste is enveloped in each of the tender cakes.
—Deirdre Dee Cox, Milwaukee, Wisconsin

      4 cups all-purpose flour
    1/2 cup sugar
      2 packages (1/4 ounce *each*) active dry yeast
      1 teaspoon salt
      1 cup 2% milk
    1/2 cup butter, cubed
      2 eggs
    1/2 cup cold butter
ALMOND PASTE:
      2 cups finely chopped blanched almonds
      2 cups confectioners' sugar
      2 egg whites
    1/4 teaspoon almond extract
FINISHING:
      1 egg white, lightly beaten
      1 egg yolk
      1 tablespoon water
    1/4 cup sliced almonds

1. In a large bowl, combine 1-1/2 cups flour, sugar, yeast and salt. In a small saucepan, heat the milk and cubed butter to 120°-130°. Add to dry ingredients; beat just until moistened. Add the eggs; beat until smooth. Stir in enough remaining flour to form a firm dough. Cover and refrigerate for 8 hours or overnight.

2. Turn onto a heavily floured surface; roll the dough into an 18-in. x 12-in. rectangle. Cut the cold butter into thin slices. Starting with a short side of dough, arrange half of the butter slices over two-thirds of rectangle to within 1/2 in. of edges.

3. Fold the unbuttered third of dough over the middle third. Fold the remaining third over the middle, forming a 12-in. x 6-in. rectangle. Press edges to seal. Cover and refrigerate for 30 minutes. Roll dough into an 18-in. x 12-in. rectangle.

4. Repeat steps of dough folding, ending with a 12-in. x 6-in. rectangle, chilling and rolling dough into an 18-in. x 12-in. rectangle three times.

5. In a small bowl, combine almonds, confectioners' sugar, egg whites and extract. Set aside. On a floured surface roll dough into a 20-in. square. Cut in half, forming two rectangles.

6. Spoon half of the almond paste over one rectangle. Roll up jelly-roll style, starting with a long side. Brush edge with egg white; pinch seam to seal. Bring the ends of roll toward the center to form a "B" shape. Place seam side down on a parchment paper-lined baking sheet. Repeat with remaining dough and almond paste.

7. Cover and let rise in a warm place until doubled, about 40 minutes. Combine egg yolk and water; brush over dough. Sprinkle with sliced almonds.

8. Bake at 350° for 25-30 minutes or until golden brown. Remove from the pans to wire racks to cool. **Yield:** 2 loaves (12 slices each).

Almond Danish Coffee Cakes

Moist Apple Muffins

If you're always on the go during the holiday season, give these fruit-filled bites a try. They make a terrific snack and the perfect take-along treat for the busy days leading up to Christmas.
—*Jeanne Sherry, Putnam Valley, New York*

    1/2 cup butter, softened
1-3/4 cups packed brown sugar
    2 eggs
1-1/3 cups buttermilk
2-2/3 cups all-purpose flour
1-3/4 teaspoons ground cinnamon
    1 teaspoon baking soda
    1/8 teaspoon salt
    2 cups chopped peeled apples
    1 medium apple, peeled and cut into 24 slices
TOPPING:
    1/3 cup all-purpose flour
    1/4 cup packed brown sugar
    1/4 teaspoon ground cinnamon
    2 tablespoons cold butter

1. In a large bowl, beat butter and brown sugar until crumbly, about 2 minutes. Add the eggs, one at a time, beating well after each addition. Stir in the buttermilk. Combine the flour, cinnamon, baking soda and salt; add to the butter mixture just until moistened. Fold in chopped apples.

2. Fill paper-lined muffin cups three-fourths full. Place sliced apples over batter. For the topping, combine the flour, brown sugar and cinnamon; cut in the butter until crumbly. Sprinkle over tops.

3. Bake at 350° for 20-25 minutes or until a toothpick comes out clean. Cool for 5 minutes before removing from pans to wire racks. Serve warm. **Yield:** 2 dozen.

Moist Apple Muffins

Mocha Chip Hazelnut Scones

Scrumptious with breakfast or afternoon coffee, these little rounds boast toasted chopped hazelnuts and mini chocolate chips.
—*Sharon Gerow, Belleville, Ontario*

4-1/2 teaspoons instant coffee granules
    1 cup 2% milk
2-1/2 cups all-purpose flour
    2/3 cup packed brown sugar
    3 teaspoons baking powder
    1/2 cup cold butter
    1 cup chopped hazelnuts, toasted
    2/3 cup miniature semisweet chocolate chips

1. Dissolve the instant coffee granules in the milk; set the mixture aside.

2. In a large bowl, combine the flour, brown sugar and baking powder. Cut in butter until mixture resembles coarse crumbs. Stir milk mixture into crumb mixture just until moistened. Stir in hazelnuts and chocolate chips. Turn onto a floured surface; knead 10 times.

3. Drop by 1/4 cupfuls 2 in. apart onto greased baking sheets. Bake at 400° for 12-15 minutes or until golden brown. Serve warm. **Yield:** 16 scones.

Lemon Swirl Coffee Cake

My husband and I like to take gifts of goodies to family, friends and neighbors at Christmastime. With a sweet-tart lemon filling and drizzled glaze, this coffee cake is always well received.
—*Loraine Meyer, Bend, Oregon*

    2 packages (1/4 ounce *each*) active dry yeast
    1/2 cup warm 2% milk (110° to 115°)
    1/4 cup warm water (110° to 115°)
    2/3 cup butter, softened
    1/3 cup sugar
    2 teaspoons grated lemon peel
1-1/2 teaspoons vanilla extract
    3/4 teaspoon salt
    1/4 teaspoon ground nutmeg
    4 cups all-purpose flour
    4 eggs
FILLING:
    1/3 cup sugar
    2 tablespoons grated lemon peel
GLAZE:
    1 cup confectioners' sugar
    2 teaspoons butter, softened
    1/2 teaspoon grated lemon peel
    4 to 6 teaspoons lemon juice

1. In a large bowl, dissolve yeast in warm milk and water. Add the butter, sugar, lemon peel, vanilla, salt, nutmeg and 2 cups flour. Beat until smooth. Add eggs, one at a time, beating after each addition. Stir in enough remaining flour to form a firm dough. Do not knead.

2. Place dough in a greased bowl, turning once to grease the top. Cover and let rise in a warm place until doubled, about 1 hour. In a small bowl, combine sugar and lemon peel. Stir

dough down. Spoon a third of the dough into a greased and floured 10-in. fluted tube pan. Sprinkle with half of the sugar mixture. Repeat layers. Top with remaining dough. Cover and let rise until doubled, about 35 minutes.

3. Bake at 350° for 30-35 minutes or until golden brown. Cool for 10 minutes before removing from pan to a wire rack.

4. For the glaze, in a small bowl, combine the confectioners' sugar, butter, lemon peel and enough lemon juice to achieve desired consistency. Drizzle over cake. Serve warm. Yield: 12 servings.

Spiced Potato Doughnuts

Your guests may feel a bit nostalgic when they take a bite of these old-fashioned, fried treats. Hints of cinnamon, nutmeg and citrus make the homemade potato doughnuts hard to resist.
—June Jones, Harveyville, Kansas

    2 cups mashed potatoes (without added milk and butter)
    2 eggs
1-1/4 cups sugar
    2/3 cup buttermilk
    1/4 cup butter, melted
    1 tablespoon grated lemon peel
    4 cups all-purpose flour
    3 teaspoons baking powder
    2 teaspoons salt
    2 teaspoons ground nutmeg
    1/4 teaspoon baking soda
Oil for deep-fat frying
TOPPING:
    1/2 cup sugar
1-1/2 teaspoons ground cinnamon

1. In a large bowl, beat the potatoes, eggs, sugar, buttermilk, butter and lemon peel until blended. Combine flour, baking powder, salt, nutmeg and baking soda; gradually beat into the potato mixture and mix well.

2. Turn onto a lightly floured surface; roll to 1/2-in. thickness. Cut with a floured 2-1/2-in. doughnut cutter. In an electric skillet or deep fryer, heat oil to 375°. Fry doughnuts, a few at a time, until golden brown on both sides. Drain on paper towels. Combine sugar and cinnamon; roll warm doughnuts in mixture. Yield: 2-1/2 dozen.

Pumpkin Eggnog Rolls

When I needed to use up some eggnog, I swapped it for the milk in my sweet roll recipe. Even people who normally don't care for eggnog go back for seconds of these frosted pumpkin rolls.
—Rebecca Soske, Douglas, Wyoming

4-1/2 cups all-purpose flour
    1/2 cup sugar
    1 package (1/4 ounce) active dry yeast
    1/2 teaspoon salt
    3/4 cup eggnog
    1/2 cup butter, cubed

Pumpkin Eggnog Rolls

    1/4 cup canned pumpkin
    2 eggs
FILLING:
    1/4 cup butter, melted
    1/2 cup sugar
    1 teaspoon ground cardamom
    1 teaspoon ground allspice
FROSTING:
    2 ounces cream cheese, softened
    2 tablespoons eggnog
    1 tablespoon canned pumpkin
    1/4 teaspoon ground cardamom
    2 cups confectioners' sugar

1. In a large bowl, combine 2 cups flour, sugar, yeast and salt. In a small saucepan, heat the eggnog, butter and pumpkin to 120°-130°. Add to dry ingredients; beat on medium speed for 2 minutes. Add eggs and 1/2 cup flour; beat 3 minutes longer. Stir in enough remaining flour to form a firm dough.

2. Turn dough onto a floured surface; knead until smooth and elastic, about 6-8 minutes. Place in a greased bowl, turning once to grease the top. Cover and let rise in a warm place until doubled, about 1 hour. Punch dough down.

3. Roll into an 18-in. x 12-in. rectangle. Brush with melted butter. Combine the sugar, cardamom and allspice. Sprinkle to within 1/2 in. of edges. Roll up jelly-roll style, starting with a long side; pinch seams to seal. Cut into 1-1/2-in. slices.

4. Place the rolls, cut side down, in a greased 13-in. x 9-in. baking pan. Cover and let rise in a warm place until doubled, about 45 minutes. Bake at 350° for 20-25 minutes or until golden brown.

5. In a small bowl, beat the cream cheese, eggnog, pumpkin and cardamom until blended. Add confectioners' sugar; beat until smooth. Spread over warm rolls. Cool on a wire rack. Yield: 1 dozen.

Editor's Note: This recipe was tested with commercially prepared eggnog.

Barbecued Party Starters

Whether your Christmastime party is casual or fancy, you'll make it sparkle when you serve these scrumptious hors d'oeuvres, irresistible munchies and more.

Barbecued Party Starters

These sweet and tangy bites of beef, mini hot dogs and pineapple chunks are sure to tide everyone over before dinner. At the buffet table, set out festive toothpicks to make for easy nibbling.
—*Anastasia Weiss, Punxsutawney, Pennsylvania*

    1 pound ground beef
1/4 cup finely chopped onion
    1 package (16 ounces) miniature hot dogs, drained
    1 jar (12 ounces) apricot preserves
    1 cup barbecue sauce
    1 can (20 ounces) pineapple chunks, drained

1. In a small bowl, combine beef and onion. Shape into 1-in. balls. In a large skillet, cook meatballs in batches until no longer pink; drain.

2. Transfer to a 3-qt. slow cooker; add the hot dogs, preserves and barbecue sauce. Cover and cook on high for 2-3 hours or until heated through. Stir in pineapple; heat through. **Yield:** 18 servings (1/3 cup each).

Chili Beef Dip

No last-minute preparation is needed for this warm, creamy dip. Put it together hours before your get-together, then let the slow cooker do the work until your group is ready to dig in.
—*Pat Habiger, Spearville, Kansas*

      2 pounds lean ground beef (90% lean)
      1 large onion, chopped
      1 jalapeno pepper, seeded and chopped
      2 packages (8 ounces *each*) cream cheese, cubed
      2 cans (8 ounces *each*) tomato sauce
      1 can (4 ounces) chopped green chilies
  1/2 cup grated Parmesan cheese
  1/2 cup ketchup
      2 garlic cloves, minced
  1-1/2 teaspoons chili powder
      1 teaspoon dried oregano
Tortilla chips

1. In a large skillet, brown the beef, onion and jalapeno until meat is no longer pink; drain. Transfer to a 3- or 4-qt. slow cooker. Stir in the cream cheese, tomato sauce, chilies, Parmesan cheese, ketchup, garlic, chili powder and oregano.

2. Cover dip and cook on low for 2-3 hours or until heated through. Stir; serve with chips. **Yield:** 8 cups.

Editor's Note: When cutting hot peppers, disposable gloves are recommended. Avoid touching your face.

Bacon Mushroom Roll-Ups

Wrapped in toasted white bread, these golden roll-ups combine basic ingredients—bacon, mushrooms, onion and cream cheese— with mouthwatering results. Guests can't get enough!
—*Raymonde Bourgeois, Swastika, Ontario*

    8 bacon strips, chopped
    1 medium onion, finely chopped
    1 package (8 ounces) cream cheese, softened
    1 can (4 ounces) mushroom stems and pieces, drained
  20 slices sandwich bread, crusts removed
    3 tablespoons butter, melted

1. In a small skillet, cook bacon over medium heat until crisp. Using a slotted spoon, remove to paper towels; drain, reserving 1 tablespoon drippings.

2. In the same skillet, saute onion in drippings until tender. Transfer to a small bowl; add the cream cheese, mushrooms and bacon. Stir until blended.

3. With a rolling pin, flatten bread slightly; spread each slice with 4-1/2 teaspoons filling.

4. Roll up from a long side and secure with a toothpick. Place seam side down in two ungreased 15-in. x 10-in. x 1-in. baking pans; brush with butter.

5. Broil 4 in. from the heat for 3-4 minutes or until golden brown. Discard toothpicks. **Yield:** 20 appetizers.

Bacon Mushroom Roll-Ups

Sausage Cheesecake Appetizer

Loaded with Italian sausage, this hearty spread looks scrumptious and tastes even better. Cutting wedges is a tidy way to serve it.
—Kendra Doss, Kansas City, Missouri

  1/2 cup seasoned bread crumbs
  1/4 cup shredded Parmesan cheese
  2 tablespoons butter, melted
FILLING:
  1 jar (7 ounces) oil-packed sun-dried tomatoes
  1 pound bulk Italian sausage
  3 garlic cloves, minced
  2 packages (8 ounces *each*) cream cheese, softened
  1/4 cup heavy whipping cream
  3 eggs, lightly beaten
1-1/2 cups (6 ounces) shredded part-skim mozzarella
    cheese
  8 green onions, sliced
  1 tablespoon minced fresh basil *or* 1 teaspoon dried
    basil
Assorted crackers

1. In a small bowl, combine the bread crumbs, cheese and butter. Press onto the bottom of a greased 9-in. springform pan. Place pan on a baking sheet. Bake at 350° for 10 minutes. Cool on a wire rack.

2. Meanwhile, drain tomatoes, reserving 1 tablespoon oil. Chop enough tomatoes to measure 1/2 cup and set aside. (Save remaining tomatoes for another use.) In a large skillet, cook sausage over medium heat until no longer pink; drain. Add garlic; cook 1 minute longer.

3. In a large bowl, beat the cream cheese, cream and reserved tomato oil until smooth. Add eggs; beat on low speed just until combined. Stir in mozzarella cheese, onions, basil, sausage mixture and tomatoes. Pour over crust. Return to baking sheet. Bake for 35-40 minutes or until center is almost set.

4. Cool on a wire rack for 10 minutes. Carefully run a knife around edge of pan to loosen; cool 1 hour longer. Refrigerate overnight. Remove sides of pan. Serve at room temperature with crackers. **Yield:** 24 servings.

Sugared Curry Pecans

These sweet-spicy nuts are great for entertaining. You could also pack them in gift bags. *—Norma Granley, Ronan, Montana*

  1/4 cup sugar
  2 tablespoons honey
  1 tablespoon olive oil
  1 teaspoon ground ginger
  1 teaspoon curry powder
  1/4 to 1/2 teaspoon cayenne pepper
  3 cups pecan halves
  1/4 teaspoon salt

1. In a large microwave-safe bowl, combine the first six ingredients; microwave, uncovered, on high for 15 seconds. Add pecans; toss to coat.

2. Microwave pecans, uncovered, 3-4 minutes longer or until lightly browned, stirring after each minute. Spread onto waxed paper to cool. Sprinkle with salt. Store in an airtight container. **Yield:** about 3 cups.

Editor's Note: This recipe was tested in a 1,100-watt microwave.

Caramel Eggnog

Flavored with caramel and nutmeg, this yummy beverage from our Test Kitchen staff is a delightful spin on the holiday classic.

  1 cup sugar
  1/4 cup water
  4 cups 2% milk
  6 eggs
  2 teaspoons vanilla extract
  1/2 teaspoon ground nutmeg
  1/2 cup heavy whipping cream
Freshly grated nutmeg, optional

1. In a small saucepan, combine sugar and water. Bring to a boil. Cook and stir over medium heat until sugar is dissolved. Increase heat to medium-high. Cook without stirring until mixture turns an amber color and a candy thermometer reads 300° (hard-crack stage). Remove from the heat; gradually stir in milk.

2. In a small bowl, whisk the eggs. Whisk a small amount of hot milk mixture into eggs; return all to the pan, stirring constantly. Cook and stir over medium heat until mixture is thickened and coats the back of a spoon.

3. Pour into a large bowl; stir in vanilla and nutmeg. Place bowl in an ice-water bath, stirring frequently until cooled. Refrigerate until chilled.

4. Before serving, whip cream until soft peaks form; fold into eggnog. Top servings with nutmeg if desired. **Yield:** 8 servings.

Sausage Cheesecake Appetizer

Raspberry Sparkle Punch

Refreshing and festive, this berry punch always goes over well. Try it at everything from a Christmas party to a bridal shower.
—Tammy Logan, Oak Ridge, Tennessee

    2 packages (10 ounces *each*) frozen sweetened
        raspberries, thawed
    4 cups cold water
    1 can (12 ounces) frozen lemonade concentrate,
        thawed
    2 liters diet lemon-lime soda, chilled

Place berries in a blender; cover and process until blended. Strain and discard seeds and pulp. Pour juice into a punch bowl; stir in water and lemonade concentrate. Just before serving, stir in soda. **Yield:** 32 servings (3/4 cup each).

Spiced Chicken Wings

Be prepared for recipe requests when you serve a platter of these crispy baked wings. They have just the right amount of heat.
—Jan Stawara, Howell, Michigan

    1/2 cup all-purpose flour
      2 teaspoons garlic powder
      1 teaspoon garlic salt
      1 teaspoon *each* ground mustard, ginger and nutmeg
    1/2 teaspoon pepper
    1/2 teaspoon ground allspice
    1/2 teaspoon cayenne pepper
     12 whole chicken wings (2-1/2 pounds)
    1/3 cup butter, melted

1. In a large resealable plastic bag, combine the flour, garlic powder, garlic salt, mustard, ginger, nutmeg, pepper, allspice and cayenne.

2. Cut chicken wings into three sections; discard wing tip sections. Dip chicken in butter, then add chicken wings, a few at a time, to flour mixture and toss to coat.

3. Arrange wings in a single layer in an ungreased 15-in. x 10-in. x 1-in. baking pan. Bake, uncovered, at 400° for 35-40 minutes or until chicken juices run clear. Broil 3-4 in. from the heat for 4-6 minutes or until golden brown. **Yield:** 2 dozen.

Editor's Note: Uncooked chicken wing sections (wingettes) may be substituted for whole chicken wings.

Butterflied Shrimp Rockefeller

Looking for an alternative to heavy holiday fare? These elegant, refreshing shrimp bites really stand out in an appetizer spread.
—Lee Bremson, Kansas City, Missouri

     18 uncooked jumbo shrimp
      2 shallots, finely chopped
      1 teaspoon dried basil
    1/2 teaspoon fennel seed, crushed
    1/4 teaspoon pepper
      1 tablespoon olive oil
      1 garlic clove, minced

Butterflied Shrimp Rockefeller

      1 package (9 ounces) fresh baby spinach, chopped
    1/2 cup dry bread crumbs
      1 tablespoon lemon juice
      1 tablespoon grated Parmesan cheese

1. Peel and devein shrimp, leaving the tails on. Butterfly each shrimp along the outside curve; set aside.

2. In a large skillet, saute the shallots, basil, fennel seed and pepper in oil until tender. Add garlic; saute for 1 minute. Add spinach; saute 3-4 minutes longer or until wilted. Remove from the heat; stir in bread crumbs and lemon juice.

3. Arrange shrimp on a greased 15-in. x 10-in. x 1-in. baking pan. Spoon 1 tablespoon spinach mixture over each shrimp; sprinkle with cheese. Bake at 425° for 4-6 minutes or until shrimp turn pink. **Yield:** 1-1/2 dozen.

Tortilla Pizza Wedges

My lighter version of pizza rolls, these get raves from adults and kids alike. Plus, the layered wedges travel very well.
—Rosemarie Weleski, Natrona Heights, Pennsylvania

      1 package (8 ounces) reduced-fat cream cheese
      1 cup (8 ounces) reduced-fat sour cream
      1 cup (4 ounces) shredded part-skim mozzarella
        cheese
      1 small onion, finely chopped
    1/2 cup finely chopped sweet red pepper
    1/2 cup sliced pepperoni, finely chopped
      1 teaspoon Italian seasoning
      8 whole wheat tortillas (8 inches)
      1 can (15 ounces) pizza sauce, warmed

1. In a large bowl, beat cream cheese and sour cream until smooth. Stir in the mozzarella cheese, onion, pepper, pepperoni and Italian seasoning.

2. Place two tortillas on a pan; spread each with 1/2 cup cheese mixture. Repeat layers twice. Top each with remaining tortillas. Cover and refrigerate for at least 1 hour. Cut each into 16 wedges. Serve with pizza sauce. **Yield:** 32 servings.

Carrie's Famous Turkey

Christmas Dinner

Gather loved ones around your holiday table for favorites such as Orange-Glazed Ham, Scalloped Pineapple, Sweet Potato Hot Rolls and Cranberry Walnut Pie.

Carrie's Famous Turkey

If you're looking for a simple yet impressive bird, this is it! Moist and flavorful, the golden-brown turkey is sure to thrill guests.
—Carrie Goedken, Iowa City, Iowa

    1 turkey (14 to 16 pounds)
1/2 cup butter, softened
    4 garlic cloves, minced
    4 teaspoons minced fresh sage
    2 teaspoons minced fresh rosemary
    1 large onion, quartered
    1 medium apple, quartered
    6 fresh sage leaves
    4 fresh rosemary sprigs
1/4 cup olive oil
1/2 teaspoon salt
1/4 teaspoon pepper

1. With fingers, carefully loosen the skin from turkey breast. Combine the butter, garlic, minced sage and minced rosemary; rub under turkey skin. Secure skin to underside of breast with toothpicks.

2. Loosely stuff turkey with the onion, apple, sage leaves and rosemary sprigs. Place breast side up on a rack in a roasting pan. Brush with oil; sprinkle with salt and pepper.

3. Bake at 325° for 2-3/4 to 3-1/4 hours or until a meat thermometer reads 180°, basting occasionally with pan drippings. Cover loosely with foil if turkey browns too quickly. Cover and let stand for 20 minutes; remove and discard onion, apple and herbs before carving. **Yield:** 14 servings.

Gruyere Potatoes au Gratin

This rich and creamy side dish is easy to prepare but tastes like you fussed for hours. —Suzan Ward, Post Falls, Idaho

    1 package (30 ounces) frozen shredded hash brown
      potatoes
    2 tablespoons lemon juice
    2 garlic cloves, minced
    1 teaspoon salt
1/2 teaspoon pepper
    2 cups (8 ounces) shredded Gruyere cheese *or* Swiss
      cheese
    1 cup grated Parmesan cheese
    2 cups heavy whipping cream

1. In a large bowl, combine the hash browns, lemon juice, garlic, salt and pepper. In a small bowl, combine the Gruyere and Parmesan cheeses.

2. Layer half of the hash brown mixture and half of the cheese in a greased 13-in. x 9-in. baking dish. Repeat layers. Pour the cream over the top.

3. Cover and bake at 400° for 45 minutes. Uncover; bake 5-10 minutes longer or until the edges begin to brown. Let stand for 5 minutes before cutting. **Yield:** 12 servings (3/4 cup each).

Citrus, Avocado & Radish Salad

With oranges, radishes and red onion, this salad makes a colorful addition to a special feast. —Julia Bushree, Georgetown, Texas

    1 package (5 ounces) spring mix salad greens
    2 medium navel oranges, peeled and chopped
    1 cup sliced radishes
    1 medium ripe avocado, peeled and thinly sliced
    1 small red onion, thinly sliced
1/2 cup chopped pecans, toasted
DRESSING:
1/4 cup olive oil
    3 tablespoons lemon juice
    2 tablespoons orange juice
    2 teaspoons Dijon mustard
    1 teaspoon sugar
1/8 teaspoon salt
1/8 teaspoon pepper

1. Arrange salad greens on a serving platter; top with oranges, radishes, avocado and onion. Sprinkle with pecans.

2. In a small bowl, whisk dressing ingredients. Drizzle over salad. Serve immediately. **Yield:** 10 servings (2/3 cup dressing).

Citrus, Avocado & Radish Salad

Fancy Julienned Carrots

These fuss-free yet crowd-pleasing carrots will brighten up any holiday menu. Plus, leftovers are just as good the next day.
—Susan Perry, Honokaa, Hawaii

    1 pound carrots, julienned (6 cups)
    3/4 cup chopped green onions
    1/4 cup butter, cubed
    1/4 cup sherry, optional
    2 tablespoons minced fresh parsley
    1/8 teaspoon salt
    1/8 teaspoon pepper

In a large skillet, saute the carrots and 2/3 cup onions in butter for 4 minutes. Reduce heat; cover and cook for 8-10 minutes or until carrots are tender. Add the sherry if desired, parsley, salt and pepper; toss to coat. Sprinkle with remaining onions. Yield: 5 servings.

Apple Stuffing Muffins

Give stuffing a fun twist with these single-serving portions baked in a muffin pan. Everyone likes them—even kids! For an elegant presentation, use metallic gold or silver muffin cups.
—Tamara Huron, New Market, Alabama

    1/4 cup butter, cubed
    3 tablespoons canola oil
    1 large onion, chopped
    2 celery ribs, chopped
    3 medium apples, peeled and chopped
    1/2 teaspoon salt
    1/2 teaspoon dried rosemary, crushed
    1/2 teaspoon pepper

Apple Stuffing Muffins

    8 cups stuffing mix
    3 cups vegetable broth
    1 cup dried cranberries
    1/4 cup minced fresh parsley

1. In a large skillet over medium-high heat, heat butter and oil. Add onion and celery; cook and stir until tender. Add the apples, salt, rosemary and pepper; cook 4-6 minutes longer or until apples are tender. Remove from the heat. Stir in the stuffing mix, broth, cranberries and parsley.

2. Fill greased muffin cups with a heaping 1/2 cup scoop. Bake at 375° for 25-30 minutes or until lightly browned. Cool for 10 minutes before removing from pans. Serve warm. Yield: 14 servings.

Pomegranate & Baby Spinach Salad

I toss together greens, blue cheese, pomegranate seeds and toasted hazelnuts for this special-occasion salad. You won't want to serve it without the tongue-tingling, made-from-scratch dressing.
—Nancy Mueller, Menomonee Falls, Wisconsin

    1 package (6 ounces) fresh baby spinach
    2 cups torn Bibb lettuce
    1 cup (4 ounces) crumbled blue cheese
    1/2 cup pomegranate seeds
    1/2 cup coarsely chopped hazelnuts, toasted
DRESSING:
    2 tablespoons canola oil
    2 tablespoons pomegranate juice
    2 tablespoons balsamic vinegar
    1/2 teaspoon Dijon mustard
    1/2 teaspoon honey
    1/8 teaspoon salt
    1/8 teaspoon pepper

1. In a salad bowl, combine the spinach, lettuce, blue cheese, pomegranate seeds and hazelnuts.

2. In a small bowl, whisk the dressing ingredients. Drizzle over spinach mixture; toss to coat. Serve immediately. Yield: 8 servings.

Five-Cheese Rigatoni

This irresistible baked pasta boasts a homemade sauce that blends Swiss, fontina, mozzarella, Parmesan and Romano cheeses.
—Shirley Foltz, Dexter, Kansas

    1 package (16 ounces) rigatoni *or* large tube pasta
    2 tablespoons butter
    3 tablespoons all-purpose flour
    1 teaspoon salt
    1/2 teaspoon pepper
2-1/2 cups whole milk
    1/2 cup shredded Swiss cheese
    1/2 cup shredded fontina cheese
    1/2 cup shredded part-skim mozzarella cheese
    1/2 cup grated Parmesan cheese, *divided*
    1/2 cup grated Romano cheese, *divided*

1. Cook rigatoni according to package directions. In a large saucepan, melt butter. Stir in the flour, salt and pepper until smooth. Gradually stir in milk; bring to a boil. Cook and stir for 1-2 minutes or until thickened. Stir in the Swiss, fontina, mozzarella, 1/4 cup Parmesan and 1/4 cup Romano cheeses until melted.

2. Drain rigatoni; stir in cheese sauce. Transfer to a greased 13-in. x 9-in. baking dish. Sprinkle with remaining cheeses. Cover and bake at 375° for 20 minutes. Uncover; bake 5-10 minutes longer or until bubbly. **Yield:** 9 servings.

Layered Cranberry Gelatin Salad

Go beyond the can with this tangy cranberry treat. Topped with a marshmallow and cream-cheese layer, it's guaranteed to please.
—Irma Senner, Dixmont, Maine

CRANBERRY LAYER:
    1 package (3 ounces) cranberry *or* raspberry gelatin
    1 cup boiling water
    1 can (14 ounces) whole-berry cranberry sauce
LEMON LAYER:
    1 package (3 ounces) lemon gelatin
    1 cup boiling water
    1 package (3 ounces) cream cheese, softened
  1/3 cup mayonnaise
    1 can (8 ounces) crushed pineapple, undrained
  1/2 cup heavy whipping cream, whipped
    1 cup miniature marshmallows
    2 tablespoons chopped pecans

1. In a small bowl, dissolve the cranberry gelatin in boiling water; stir in cranberry sauce until blended. Transfer to an 8-in. square dish. Refrigerate until set.

2. In another bowl, dissolve lemon gelatin in boiling water. Beat cream cheese and mayonnaise until smooth; stir into the lemon gelatin with the pineapple. Refrigerate until slightly thickened, about 2 hours.

3. Fold the cream, marshmallows and pecans into cream cheese mixture. Spread over cranberry layer. Refrigerate for 4 hours or until set. **Yield:** 12 servings.

Horseradish-Encrusted Beef Tenderloin

When it comes to an impressive entree, you can't beat this tender beef tenderloin encased in a golden horseradish crust.
—Laura Bagozzi, Dublin, Ohio

    1 whole garlic bulb
    1 teaspoon olive oil
  1/3 cup prepared horseradish
  1/4 teaspoon salt
  1/4 teaspoon dried basil
  1/4 teaspoon dried thyme
  1/4 teaspoon pepper

Balsamic-Glazed Parsnips & Onions
Horseradish-Encrusted Beef Tenderloin

  1/3 cup soft bread crumbs
    1 beef tenderloin roast (3 pounds)

1. Remove the papery outer skin from garlic (do not peel or separate cloves). Cut top off garlic bulb; brush with oil. Wrap in heavy-duty foil. Bake at 425° for 30-35 minutes or until softened. Cool for 10-15 minutes.

2. Squeeze the softened garlic into a small bowl; stir in the horseradish, salt, basil, thyme and pepper. Add bread crumbs; toss to coat. Spread over top of tenderloin. Place on a rack in a large shallow roasting pan.

3. Bake at 400° for 45-55 minutes or until the meat reaches the desired doneness (for medium-rare, a meat thermometer should read 145°; medium, 160°; well-done, 170°). Let stand for 10 minutes before slicing. **Yield:** 8 servings.

Balsamic-Glazed Parsnips & Onions

Brown sugar and vinegar add a sweet-tart glaze to the vegetables in this rustic side dish. It goes well with a variety of main courses.
—Marion Brown, Elgin, Illinois

    2 pounds parsnips, halved and cut into 1-inch pieces
    2 medium onions, halved and sliced
  1/4 cup packed brown sugar
  1/4 cup olive oil
  1/4 cup balsamic vinegar
  1/2 teaspoon salt
  1/2 teaspoon pepper

1. In a large bowl, combine all ingredients. Transfer to a greased 15-in. x 10-in. x 1-in. baking pan.

2. Cover and bake at 425° for 35 minutes. Uncover; bake 5-10 minutes longer or until tender. **Yield:** 6 servings.

Herbed Dinner Rolls

Herbed Dinner Rolls

Why settle for refrigerated rolls? These cheesy bites are easy to bake in a muffin pan and are absolutely delicious served warm.
—Harrison Carpenter, Longmont, Colorado

1-1/2 cups all-purpose flour
4-1/2 teaspoons herbes de Provence
   2 teaspoons baking powder
1/2 teaspoon salt
   2 eggs, beaten
   1 cup buttermilk
   1 tablespoon butter, melted
1/2 cup grated Romano cheese

1. In a large bowl, combine the flour, herbes de Provence, baking powder and salt. In another bowl, combine the eggs, buttermilk and butter. Stir into the dry ingredients just until moistened.

2. Fill greased muffin cups half full. Sprinkle with cheese. Bake at 400° for 18-20 minutes or until a toothpick inserted in a muffin comes out clean. Cool for 5 minutes before removing from pan to a wire rack. Serve warm. **Yield:** 8 rolls.

Editor's Note: Look for herbes de Provence in the spice aisle.

Orange-Glazed Ham

A citrusy, sweet-spicy glaze makes this main course extra-special. If you prefer, replace the whiskey in the recipe with apple cider.
—Laura McDowell, Lake Villa, Illinois

   1 boneless fully cooked ham (4 to 6 pounds)
1/3 cup packed brown sugar
1/3 cup whiskey *or* apple cider
   1 tablespoon grated orange peel
1/4 teaspoon ground allspice
1/8 teaspoon ground cloves

1. Place the ham on a rack in a shallow roasting pan. Cover and bake at 325° for 1-1/4 to 1-3/4 hours or until a meat thermometer reads 130°.

2. In a small saucepan, combine brown sugar, whiskey, orange peel, allspice and cloves. Bring to a boil. Reduce heat; simmer, uncovered, for 5-7 minutes or until slightly thickened.

3. Brush some of the sauce over the ham. Bake, uncovered, 20 minutes longer or until a meat thermometer reads 140°, brushing twice with sauce. Let stand for 10 minutes before slicing. **Yield:** 12 servings.

Scalloped Pineapple

This tangy side dish is a wonderful accompaniment to a holiday ham. It's also a great choice for potlucks and church suppers.
—Diana Loewen, Benton Harbor, Michigan

   3 eggs
1/2 cup sugar
1/2 cup butter, melted
1/2 cup sweetened condensed milk
   1 can (20 ounces) unsweetened crushed pineapple, undrained
   4 cups cubed bread

1. In a large bowl, whisk the eggs, sugar, butter and milk. Stir in pineapple with juice; fold in bread cubes. Transfer to a greased 8-in. square baking dish.

2. Bake, uncovered, at 350° for 40-45 minutes or until a thermometer inserted near the center reads 160°. Let stand for 10 minutes before serving. **Yield:** 8 servings.

Cranberry Walnut Pie

Everyone will save room for dessert when this one is on the menu. With a lattice crust, the home-style pie looks as good as it tastes.
—Diane Everett, Dunkirk, New York

   1 package (12 ounces) fresh *or* frozen cranberries, thawed
1-1/2 cups packed brown sugar
   1 cup chopped walnuts
1/4 cup butter, melted
4-1/2 teaspoons all-purpose flour
   2 teaspoons grated orange peel
Dash salt
Pastry for double-crust pie (9 inches)

1. Place cranberries in a food processor; cover and process until finely chopped. Transfer to a large bowl; stir in the brown sugar, walnuts, butter, flour, orange peel and salt.

2. Roll out half of pastry to fit a 9-in. pie plate; transfer pastry to pie plate. Pour filling into crust. Roll out remaining pastry; make a lattice crust. Trim, seal and flute edges. Cover edges loosely with foil.

3. Bake at 375° for 30 minutes. Remove the foil; bake 20-25 minutes longer or until filling is bubbly and crust is golden brown. Cool on a wire rack. **Yield:** 8 servings.

Cranberry Walnut Pie
Scalloped Pineapple
Orange-Glazed Ham

Classic Endive Salad

This hearty green salad is a variation of my mother's old recipe. It's so good drizzled with the accompanying dressing.
—*Penny Hamilton, Granby, Colorado*

8 bacon strips, chopped
1/4 cup balsamic vinegar
3 tablespoons honey
1/4 teaspoon ground mustard
1/4 teaspoon salt
1/4 teaspoon pepper
8 cups torn curly endive
1 pint cherry tomatoes
8 green onions, thinly sliced
1/2 cup sliced water chestnuts
1/2 cup coarsely chopped walnuts, toasted
1/2 cup salad croutons
2 hard-cooked eggs, chopped

1. In a large skillet, cook bacon over medium heat until crisp. Remove to paper towels with a slotted spoon; drain, reserving 3 tablespoons drippings. Stir the vinegar, honey, mustard, salt and pepper into drippings; heat through. Keep warm.

2. In a salad bowl, combine the endive, tomatoes, onions, water chestnuts, walnuts, croutons and bacon. Pour warm dressing over salad; toss to coat. Sprinkle with eggs. Serve immediately. **Yield: 10 servings.**

Eggnog Sweet Potato Casserole

Creamy eggnog, raisins and a crunchy pecan topping accent the sweet potatoes in this comforting Christmas side dish.
—*Katie Wollgast, Florissant, Missouri*

6 cups mashed sweet potatoes (about 3 pounds)
2/3 cup eggnog

Eggnog Sweet Potato Casserole

1/2 cup golden raisins
2 tablespoons sugar
1 teaspoon salt
TOPPING:
1/4 cup all-purpose flour
1/4 cup quick-cooking oats
1/4 cup packed brown sugar
1/4 cup chopped pecans
3 tablespoons butter, melted
3/4 teaspoon ground cinnamon
1/4 teaspoon ground nutmeg

1. In a large bowl, combine sweet potatoes, eggnog, golden raisins, sugar and salt. Transfer to a greased 2-qt. baking dish. Combine the topping ingredients; sprinkle over top.

2. Bake, uncovered, at 350° for 30-35 minutes or until heated through. **Yield: 8 servings.**

Chicken Breasts With Curry Sauce

Warm up guests on chilly evenings with this out-of-the-ordinary entree. The saucy chicken is delicious served on a bed of rice.
—*Pam Norby, Amery, Wisconsin*

1 package (6 ounces) rice pilaf
1/4 teaspoon salt
1/4 teaspoon plus 1/8 teaspoon pepper, *divided*
4 boneless skinless chicken breast halves (6 ounces *each*)
2 tablespoons olive oil
1 package (3-1/2 ounces) sliced fresh shiitake mushrooms
4 tablespoons butter, *divided*
2 large pears, peeled and sliced
2 tablespoons all-purpose flour
2 tablespoons curry powder
1 cup chicken broth
1 tablespoon mango chutney
1/2 cup heavy whipping cream
1/4 cup chopped salted peanuts
2 tablespoons minced fresh cilantro

1. Prepare the rice pilaf according to the package directions. Meanwhile, sprinkle salt and 1/4 teaspoon pepper over chicken breasts. In a large skillet over medium heat, cook chicken in oil for 4-6 minutes on each side or until a meat thermometer reads 170°. Remove and keep warm.

2. In same skillet, saute mushrooms in 2 tablespoons butter for 4 minutes; add pears. Saute 2-3 minutes longer or until mushrooms and pears are tender. Remove and keep warm.

3. In same skillet, melt the remaining butter. Stir in the flour, curry powder and remaining pepper until blended; gradually add the chicken broth and chutney. Bring to a boil. Reduce heat; simmer, uncovered, for 5-7 minutes or until thickened, stirring occasionally.

4. Gradually stir the cream into skillet; add the chicken and mushroom mixture. Heat through. Serve over rice; sprinkle with peanuts and cilantro. **Yield: 4 servings.**

Hummingbird Cheesecake

Featuring mellow banana and tangy pineapple flavors, this soft cheesecake is a rich but refreshing dessert for any feast.
—Linda Stemen, Monroeville, Indiana

     3/4 cup graham cracker crumbs
     3/4 cup toasted ground pecans
     1/4 cup butter, melted
       4 packages (8 ounces *each*) cream cheese, softened
       1 cup packed brown sugar
       1 teaspoon vanilla extract
       4 eggs, lightly beaten
       1 cup crushed pineapple, drained
     3/4 cup mashed ripe banana
TOPPING:
       1 cup heavy whipping cream
       3 tablespoons confectioners' sugar
     1/2 teaspoon vanilla extract

1. Place a greased 9-in. springform pan on a double thickness of heavy-duty foil (about 18 in. square). Securely wrap foil around pan.

2. In a small bowl, combine the cracker crumbs, pecans and butter. Press onto the bottom of prepared pan; set aside.

3. In a large bowl, beat the cream cheese and brown sugar until smooth. Beat in vanilla. Add eggs; beat on low speed just until combined. Stir in pineapple and banana. Pour into crust. Place springform pan in a large baking pan; add 1 in. of hot water to larger pan.

4. Bake at 350° for 45-50 minutes or until center is just set and top appears dull. Remove springform pan from water bath. Cool on a wire rack for 10 minutes. Carefully run a knife around edge of pan to loosen; cool 1 hour longer. Refrigerate overnight. Remove sides of pan.

5. In a small bowl, beat cream until it begins to thicken. Add confectioners' sugar and vanilla; beat until soft peaks form. Garnish cheesecake with whipped cream. **Yield:** 12 servings.

Italian-Style Onion Soup

Each bowlful of this veggie soup is crowned with a slice of cheesy, tomato-topped toast. —*Debbie Miller, Oldsmar, Florida*

       2 tablespoons butter
       1 tablespoon olive oil
       6 medium sweet onions, thinly sliced (about 6 cups)
     1/2 teaspoon minced fresh rosemary
     1/4 teaspoon salt, *divided*
     1/4 teaspoon pepper, *divided*
       6 cups beef broth
     1/2 cup white wine *or* additional beef broth
       1 tablespoon balsamic vinegar
       1 cup grape tomatoes, quartered
     1/2 cup fresh basil leaves, thinly sliced
     1/4 cup grated Parmesan cheese
     1/2 teaspoon garlic powder
       5 slices day-old French bread (1-1/2 inches thick), toasted
       5 slices part-skim mozzarella cheese

Italian-Style Onion Soup

1. In a Dutch oven over medium heat, melt the butter with the oil. Add the sweet onions, rosemary, 1/8 teaspoon salt and 1/8 teaspoon pepper. Cook for 30 minutes or until lightly browned, stirring occasionally. Add the beef broth, wine and vinegar; heat through.

2. Meanwhile, in a small bowl, combine the grape tomatoes, basil, Parmesan cheese, garlic powder and remaining salt and pepper. Spoon tomato mixture over bread slices; top with cheese. Place on a baking sheet.

3. Broil 3-4 in. from the heat for 2-3 minutes or until cheese is melted. Ladle soup into bowls; top with tomato-topped toasts. Serve immediately. **Yield:** 5 servings.

Sweet Potato Hot Rolls

Busy holiday cooks are sure to appreciate the ease of this simple recipe. The tender rolls start with a convenient packaged mix.
—Addy Kramer, Pine Island, Minnesota

       1 package (16 ounces) hot roll mix
     1/3 cup toasted wheat germ
       2 tablespoons sugar
       1 cup warm water (120° to 130°)
     3/4 cup mashed sweet potatoes
       2 tablespoons butter
       1 egg
EGG WASH:
       1 egg
       1 tablespoon water
       1 tablespoon toasted wheat germ

1. In a large bowl, combine contents of the roll mix and its yeast packet. Stir in wheat germ and sugar. Add the warm water, sweet potatoes, butter and egg; stir until dough pulls away from the sides of the bowl. Turn onto a lightly floured surface; knead for 5 minutes. Cover and let rest for 5 minutes.

2. Divide dough into 16 pieces. Shape each into a ball. Divide between two greased 9-in. round baking pans. Cover and let rise in a warm place until doubled, about 30 minutes.

3. Beat egg and water; brush over rolls. Sprinkle with wheat germ. Bake at 375° for 15-20 minutes or until golden brown. Remove to wire racks. **Yield:** 16 rolls.

Chocolate Raspberry Cake

Decadent Desserts

Watch eyes light up when you surprise Christmas guests with the home-style pies, frosted layer cakes and other delectable delights featured in this section.

Chocolate Raspberry Cake

A luscious raspberry filling and hint of coffee flavor make this moist layer cake extra special. Garnished with fresh berries and chocolate curls, it looks as if it came from a bakery!
—Tammy Bollman, Minatare, Nebraska

    2 cups sugar
    1 cup 2% milk
    1 cup strong brewed coffee
    1 cup canola oil
    2 eggs
    1 teaspoon vanilla extract
    2 cups all-purpose flour
    3/4 cup baking cocoa
    1 tablespoon instant coffee granules
    2 teaspoons baking soda
    1 teaspoon baking powder
    1 teaspoon salt
FILLING:
    1 cup butter, softened
 1-1/2 cups confectioners' sugar
    1/2 cup seedless raspberry jam
FROSTING:
    9 ounces bittersweet chocolate, chopped
 1-1/2 cups butter, softened
    3 cups marshmallow creme
    1/2 cup confectioners' sugar
    1 teaspoon vanilla extract
Fresh raspberries and chocolate curls

1. In a large bowl, beat the sugar, milk, coffee, oil, eggs and vanilla until well blended. In a small bowl, combine the flour, cocoa, coffee granules, baking soda, baking powder and salt; gradually beat into sugar mixture until blended.

2. Pour into two greased and floured 9-in. baking pans. Bake at 325° for 30-35 minutes or until a toothpick inserted near the center comes out clean. Cool for 10 minutes before removing from pans to wire racks to cool completely.

3. For filling, in a large bowl, beat butter and confectioners' sugar. Add jam; beat until blended.

4. For frosting, melt the chocolate in a microwave; stir until smooth. In a large bowl, beat butter and chocolate until fluffy. Add marshmallow creme, confectioners' sugar and extract; beat until smooth.

5. Place one cake layer on a serving plate; spread with the raspberry filling. Top with the remaining cake layer. Spread the chocolate frosting over the top and sides of cake. Garnish with fresh raspberries and chocolate curls. Store cake in the refrigerator. **Yield: 16 servings.**

Frozen Tiramisu

Java lovers are sure to cheer for this mocha treat. It's a wonderful make-ahead option.   —April Harmon, Greeneville, Tennessee

    1/4 cup strong brewed coffee
    4 teaspoons rum
    1 package (3 ounces) ladyfingers, split
 1-1/2 quarts plus 1 pint coffee ice cream, softened
    2 ounces bittersweet chocolate, grated
    1 carton (8 ounces) Mascarpone cheese
    3 tablespoons coffee liqueur
    1 tablespoon sugar
    1/3 cup half-and-half cream
Additional bittersweet chocolate, grated

1. Line a 9-in. x 5-in. loaf pan with plastic wrap, letting edges hang over sides; set aside. In a small bowl, combine coffee and rum; brush over ladyfingers. Arrange ladyfingers over bottom and around sides of prepared pan, rounded sides out.

2. In a large bowl, combine ice cream and chocolate; spread into pan. Freeze overnight or until firm.

3. For sauce, in a small bowl, combine the cheese, liqueur and sugar. Stir in cream until smooth.

4. To serve, unmold dessert, using ends of plastic wrap to lift from pan. Remove plastic. Cut into slices. Serve with sauce and garnish with additional chocolate. **Yield: 12 servings.**

Editor's Note: This recipe was prepared with Alessi brand ladyfinger cookies.

Frozen Tiramisu

Phyllo Apples with Rum Raisin Sauce

Flaky phyllo dough forms a "bowl" for these tender apples topped with a scoop of ice cream and drizzled with a delectable sauce.
—*Marie Rizzio, Interlochen, Michigan*

    6 small apples, peeled and cored
    4 sheets phyllo dough (14 inches x 9 inches)
    1/4 cup butter, melted
    1/3 cup slivered almonds, toasted
    1/4 cup sugar
    1 teaspoon ground cinnamon
    1 tablespoon cornstarch
    1/3 cup cold water
    1/2 cup packed brown sugar
    1/3 cup raisins
    1 tablespoon rum
    3 cups vanilla ice cream

1. Cut apples into wedges three-fourths of the way down, leaving bottoms intact; place in an 11-in. x 7-in. baking dish. Microwave, uncovered, on high for 5 minutes or just until apples begin to soften.

2. Grease six 4-oz. ramekins; set aside. Brush one sheet phyllo dough with butter; layer with remaining sheets and butter. Cut the stack lengthwise into six strips and widthwise into thirds, creating eighteen strips. Layer three strips in a greased 4-oz. ramekin, allowing ends to hang over edge. Top with an apple. Repeat.

3. Fill apples with almonds. Combine sugar and cinnamon; sprinkle over apples. Place ramekins in a 15-in. x 10-in. x 1-in. baking pan. Bake at 375° for 18-22 minutes or until golden brown. Cool slightly.

4. In a small heavy saucepan, combine cornstarch and water until smooth. Stir in brown sugar and raisins. Cook and stir over medium heat until thickened and bubbly. Remove from the heat; stir in rum.

5. Carefully slip phyllo apples out of the ramekins and onto dessert plates. Top with ice cream; drizzle with sauce. Serve immediately. Yield: 6 servings.

Editor's Note: This recipe was tested in a 1,100-watt microwave.

Butter-Crust Apple Pie

My father loves apple pie, and I've been baking them since I was a girl. The buttery crust and spices in this one make it stand out.
—*Courtney Irwin, Reno, Nevada*

    4 cups all-purpose flour
    1/4 cup sugar
    1-1/2 cups cold butter
    6 to 8 tablespoons cold water
FILLING:
    12 cups thinly sliced peeled tart apples
    1/2 cup sugar
    1/2 cup packed brown sugar
    3 tablespoons molasses
    2 tablespoons all-purpose flour
    1-1/4 teaspoons ground cinnamon
    1 teaspoon ground ginger
    1/2 teaspoon ground nutmeg
    1/2 teaspoon ground cloves
EGG WASH:
    1 egg white
    1 teaspoon water

1. In a large bowl, combine flour and sugar; cut in butter until crumbly. Gradually add water, tossing with a fork until dough forms a ball. Divide dough in fourths so that two portions are slightly larger than the other two; wrap each in plastic wrap. Refrigerate for 1 hour or until easy to handle.

2. In a large bowl, combine the apples, sugar, brown sugar, molasses, flour and spices. Roll out one larger portion of dough to fit a 9-in. pie plate. Transfer pastry to plate. Trim pastry even with edge. Spoon half of filling into crust. Repeat with remaining large portion of dough and filling.

3. Roll out remaining pastry to fit tops of pies. Place over filling. Trim, seal and flute edges. Cut slits in pastry. Beat egg white and water; brush over pastry.

4. Bake at 375° for 55-65 minutes or until the crust is golden brown. Cool on a wire rack. Yield: 2 pies (8 servings each).

Cranberry-Pecan Pound Cake

With tangy cranberries and crunchy pecans, this pound cake is a seasonal delight. —*Lisa Varner, Charleston, South Carolina*

    1 cup butter, softened
    1 package (8 ounces) cream cheese, softened
    1-1/2 cups sugar
    4 eggs
    2 teaspoons vanilla extract
    2-1/4 cups all-purpose flour
    3 teaspoons baking powder
    1/2 teaspoon salt

Phyllo Apples with Rum Raisin Sauce

1/2 teaspoon grated orange peel
1/2 cup dried cranberries
1/2 cup chopped pecans
  1 tablespoon confectioners' sugar

1. In a large bowl, cream the butter, cream cheese and sugar until light and fluffy. Add the eggs, one at a time, beating well after each addition. Beat in vanilla. Combine the flour, baking powder, salt and orange peel; gradually beat into creamed mixture. Fold in cranberries and pecans.

2. Transfer to a greased and floured 10-in. fluted tube pan. Bake at 325° for 50-60 minutes or until a toothpick inserted near the center comes out clean. Cool for 10 minutes before removing from pan to a wire rack to cool completely. Dust with confectioners' sugar. **Yield:** 12 servings.

Caramel-Apple Cheesecake Bars

These nutty bars are especially good during the fall and winter months, when you're craving something rich and satisfying.
—Katy Roche, Batavia, Illinois

1-1/4 cups graham cracker crumbs
  1/2 cup chopped pecans, toasted
  1/2 cup butter, melted
    3 tablespoons brown sugar
APPLE LAYER:
    4 cups thinly sliced peeled tart apples
  1/4 cup all-purpose flour
    1 tablespoon sugar
CREAM CHEESE LAYER:
    1 package (8 ounces) cream cheese, softened
  3/4 cup sugar
    3 tablespoons sour cream
    1 teaspoon vanilla extract
    2 eggs, lightly beaten
CARAMEL LAYER:
    1 package (14 ounces) caramels
  1/3 cup 2% milk
TOPPING:
    1 cup chopped pecans, toasted
  2/3 cup all-purpose flour
  1/3 cup packed brown sugar
    5 tablespoons butter, melted

1. In a small bowl, combine crumbs, pecans, butter and brown sugar. Press onto bottom of a well-greased 13-in. x 9-in. baking pan. Bake at 350° for 8-10 minutes. Cool on a wire rack.

2. In a small bowl, combine the apples, flour and sugar; spoon over crust. In a small bowl, beat cream cheese and sugar until smooth. Beat in sour cream and vanilla. Add eggs; beat on low speed just until combined. Pour over apples.

3. In a small saucepan, combine caramels and milk. Cook and stir over medium heat until smooth; pour over cream cheese layer. In a small bowl, combine topping ingredients; sprinkle over caramel.

4. Bake at 350° for 35-40 minutes or until center is almost set. Cool on a wire rack for 1 hour. Cover and refrigerate for at least 2 hours. Cut into bars. **Yield:** 2 dozen.

Pumpkin Torte

Pumpkin Torte

A local newspaper published this potluck-friendly recipe. It's a creamy alternative to the usual pumpkin pie served on holidays.
—Peggy Shea, Lowell, Indiana

1-2/3 cups graham cracker crumbs
  1/3 cup sugar
  1/2 cup butter, melted
CREAM CHEESE FILLING:
    2 packages (8 ounces *each*) cream cheese, softened
  3/4 cup sugar
    2 eggs, lightly beaten
PUMPKIN FILLING:
    2 envelopes unflavored gelatin
  1/2 cup cold water
    1 can (30 ounces) pumpkin pie filling
    1 can (5-1/2 ounces) evaporated milk
    2 eggs, lightly beaten
TOPPING:
    1 carton (12 ounces) frozen whipped topping, thawed

1. In a small bowl, combine the crumbs, sugar and butter. Press onto the bottom of an ungreased 13-in. x 9-in. baking dish; set aside. In a large bowl, beat cream cheese and sugar until smooth. Add eggs; beat on low speed just until combined. Pour into crust. Bake at 350° for 25-30 minutes or until center is almost set.

2. Meanwhile, in a small bowl, sprinkle gelatin over the cold water; let stand for 1 minute. In a large saucepan, combine pie filling and evaporated milk. Bring to a boil. Add gelatin; stir until dissolved. Whisk a small amount of hot mixture into the remaining eggs. Return all to the pan, whisking constantly. Cook and stir over low heat until mixture is thickened and coats the back of a spoon. Cool for 10 minutes.

3. Spread the pumpkin mixture over the cream cheese layer. Spread whipped topping over the top. Cover and refrigerate overnight. Refrigerate leftovers. **Yield:** 15 servings.

Lemon-Ginger Creme Brulee

Lemon-Ginger Creme Brulee

Everyone raves about this twist on the classic custard treat. Tangy lemon and zippy ginger add a new, tongue-tingling dimension.
—Scott Hunter, Sherman Oaks, California

    2 cups heavy whipping cream
1/3 cup plus 2 tablespoons sugar, *divided*
1/2 teaspoon ground ginger
    8 egg yolks, beaten
    1 teaspoon lemon extract
1/2 teaspoon vanilla extract
    2 tablespoons brown sugar

1. In a large heavy saucepan, heat the cream, 1/3 cup sugar and ginger until bubbles form around sides of pan. Remove from the heat; stir a small amount of hot mixture into egg yolks. Return all to the pan, stirring constantly. Stir in extracts.

2. Transfer to six 6-oz. ramekins or custard cups. Place in a baking pan; add 1 in. of boiling water to pan. Bake, uncovered, at 325° for 25-30 minutes or until the centers are just set (the mixture will jiggle). Remove ramekins from water bath; cool for 10 minutes. Cover and refrigerate for at least 4 hours.

3. Combine brown sugar and remaining sugar. If using a creme brulee torch, sprinkle custards with sugar mixture. Heat sugar with the torch until caramelized. Serve immediately.

4. If broiling the custards, place ramekins on a baking sheet; let stand at room temperature for 15 minutes. Sprinkle with sugar mixture. Broil 8 in. from the heat for 4-7 minutes or until sugar is caramelized. Refrigerate for 1-2 hours or until firm. **Yield:** 6 servings.

Spumoni Baked Alaska

For a refreshing end to a rich holiday meal, try this freezer finale created by our Test Kitchen pros. Its cool layers and Christmasy color scheme are bound to garner oohs and aahs.

1/2 cup butter, cubed
    2 ounces unsweetened chocolate, chopped
    1 cup sugar
    1 teaspoon vanilla extract
    2 eggs
3/4 cup all-purpose flour
1/2 teaspoon baking powder
1/2 teaspoon salt
    1 cup chopped hazelnuts
    2 quarts vanilla ice cream, softened, *divided*
1/2 cup chopped pistachios
1/2 teaspoon almond extract
    6 drops green food coloring, optional
1/3 cup chopped maraschino cherries
    1 tablespoon maraschino cherry juice
    1 tablespoon rum
MERINGUE:
    8 egg whites
    1 cup sugar
    1 teaspoon cream of tartar

1. In a microwave-safe bowl, melt the butter and chocolate; stir until smooth. Stir in sugar and vanilla. Add eggs, one at a time, beating well after each addition. Combine the flour, baking powder and salt; gradually stir into chocolate mixture. Stir in hazelnuts.

2. Spread batter into a greased 8-in. round baking pan. Bake at 350° for 35-40 minutes or until a toothpick inserted near the center comes out with moist crumbs (do not overbake). Cool for 10 minutes before removing from the pan to a wire rack to cool completely.

3. Meanwhile, line an 8-in. round bowl (1-1/2 qts.) with foil. In a small bowl, place 1 quart ice cream; add the pistachios, almond extract and food coloring if desired. Quickly spread ice cream over bottom and up sides of bowl, leaving center hollow; cover and freeze for 30 minutes.

4. In a small bowl, combine the cherries, cherry juice, rum and remaining ice cream. Pack ice cream into center; cover and freeze.

5. In a large heavy saucepan, combine the egg whites, sugar and cream of tartar. With a hand mixer, beat on low speed for 1 minute. Continue beating over low heat until egg mixture reaches 160°, about 8 minutes. Transfer to a bowl; beat until stiff glossy peaks form and sugar is dissolved.

6. Place cooled brownie on an ungreased foil-lined baking sheet; top with the inverted ice cream mold. Remove the foil. Immediately spread the meringue over ice cream, sealing to the edges of the brownie. Freeze until ready to serve, up to 24 hours.

7. Bake at 400° for 2-5 minutes or until meringue is lightly browned. Transfer to a serving plate; serve immediately. **Yield:** 12 servings.

Spumoni Baked Alaska

Ultimate Caramel Chocolate Popcorn

Gifts from the Kitchen

Store-bought treats just can't compete with Milky Way Crispy Bars, Pumpkin Butter, Mixed Citrus Marmalade and other homemade-from-the-heart goodies.

Ultimate Caramel Chocolate Popcorn

Snack fans will snatch up handful after handful of this nutty corn drizzled with melted chocolate. It truly is the ultimate!
—*Kim Forni, Claremont, New Hampshire*

  18 cups air-popped popcorn
   1 can (17 ounces) mixed nuts
   2 cups packed brown sugar
 1/2 cup light corn syrup
 1/2 cup butter, cubed
   1 teaspoon salt
   1 teaspoon baking soda
1-1/2 cups dark chocolate, milk chocolate *and/or* white baking chips
   3 teaspoons shortening

1. Place popcorn and nuts in a greased roasting pan; set aside. In a large heavy saucepan, combine the brown sugar, corn syrup, butter and salt. Bring to a boil over medium heat; cook and stir for 5 minutes.

2. Remove from the heat; stir in baking soda (mixture will foam). Quickly pour over popcorn and mix well.

3. Transfer the mixture to two greased 15-in. x 10-in. x 1-in. baking pans. Bake at 250° for 1 hour or until dry, stirring every 15 minutes. In a microwave, melt each chocolate separately, adding 1 teaspoon shortening to each 1/2 cup chips; stir until smooth. Drizzle over popcorn mixture; let stand until set.

4. Break into clusters. Store in an airtight container. **Yield:** 5 quarts.

Paprika Dry Rub

A friend shared this wonderful recipe with me. I love the punch of flavor it gives poultry. —*Jackie Kohn, Duluth, Minnesota*

1/2 cup sugar
1/3 cup kosher salt
1/3 cup garlic salt
1/3 cup packed brown sugar
1/3 cup paprika
  1 teaspoon dried oregano
  1 teaspoon ground cumin
  1 teaspoon coarsely ground pepper
  1 teaspoon cayenne pepper

In a small bowl, combine all ingredients. Store in an airtight container in a cool dry place for up to 1 year. Use as a rub for turkey or chicken. **Yield:** about 1-3/4 cups.

Cherry-Nut Cookies

Featuring dried cherries and pecans, these slice-and-bake cookies look and taste yummy. Plus, the dough freezes well.
—*Amy Briggs, Gove, Kansas*

   1 cup butter, softened
   1 cup sugar
   2 eggs
   1 teaspoon almond extract
3-3/4 cups all-purpose flour
   2 teaspoons baking powder
 1/4 cup heavy whipping cream
 1/2 cup dried cherries *or* cherry-flavored dried cranberries, chopped
 1/2 cup chopped pecans

1. In a large bowl, cream butter and sugar until light and fluffy. Beat in eggs and extract. Combine flour and baking powder; add half to creamed mixture and mix well. Beat in cream, then remaining flour mixture. Stir in cherries and pecans.

2. Shape into two 8-in. logs; wrap in plastic wrap. Refrigerate for 2 hours or until firm.

3. Unwrap and cut into 1/4-in. slices. Place 2 in. apart on greased baking sheets. Bake at 350° for 9-11 minutes or until lightly browned. Cool for 1 minute before removing from pans to wire racks. **Yield:** 5 dozen.

Cherry-Nut Cookies

Milky Way Crispy Bars

What's not to love about the combination of Milky Way candy bars and Rice Krispies? That's just what you get in these sweet treats.
—*Phyl Broich-Wessling, Garner, Iowa*

6 cups Rice Krispies
1 cup chopped pecans
6 Milky Way candy bars (2.05 ounces *each*), chopped
3/4 cup butter, cubed
1/2 cup white baking chips
1/2 teaspoon shortening

1. In a large bowl, combine cereal and pecans; set aside. In a large microwave-safe bowl, combine candy bars and butter. Microwave, uncovered, on high for 1-1/2 to 2 minutes or until smooth, stirring once. Stir into cereal mixture.

2. Transfer to a greased 13-in. x 9-in. pan; press down firmly. In a microwave, melt chips and shortening; stir until smooth. Drizzle over the top. Cool. Cut into bars. Store in an airtight container. Yield: 2 dozen.

Pumpkin Butter

This spiced butter is heavenly on toast or a biscuit. If you added whipped cream, you might think you were eating pumpkin pie!
—*June Barrus, Springville, Utah*

3 cans (15 ounces *each*) solid-pack pumpkin
2 cups sugar
1-1/2 cups water
3 tablespoons lemon juice
1 tablespoon grated lemon peel
3 teaspoons ground cinnamon
3/4 teaspoon salt
3/4 teaspoon ground nutmeg
3/4 teaspoon ground ginger

Pumpkin Butter

1. In a large saucepan, combine all ingredients. Bring to a boil, stirring frequently. Reduce heat; cover and simmer for 20 minutes to allow flavors to blend.

2. Cool. Spoon into jars. Cover and store in the refrigerator for up to 3 weeks. Yield: 6 cups.

Cranberry Ketchup

My mother handed down this cranberry condiment recipe to me. The unusual blend of ingredients may seem strange, but once you give it a try, you may not want to go back to regular ketchup!
—*Jerome Wiese, Bemidji, Minnesota*

1 package (12 ounces) fresh *or* frozen cranberries
1 large red onion, chopped
2 cups water
3/4 cup sugar
1/2 cup cider vinegar
1-1/2 teaspoons salt
1 cinnamon stick (3 inches)
4 whole allspice
1/2 teaspoon mustard seed
1/2 teaspoon whole peppercorns

1. In a large saucepan, combine the cranberries, red onion and water. Cook over medium heat until the cranberries pop, about 15 minutes.

2. Transfer cranberries to a food processor; cover and process until smooth. Return to the pan and bring to a boil. Reduce heat to medium-low. Cook, uncovered, for 20 minutes or until mixture is reduced to 2 cups, stirring frequently.

3. Stir in the sugar, vinegar and salt. Place the cinnamon, allspice, mustard seed and peppercorns on a double thickness of cheesecloth; bring up corners of cloth and tie with string to form a bag. Add to the cranberry mixture. Cook and stir for 25-30 minutes or until thickened.

4. Discard the spice bag. Cool the ketchup. Store ketchup in an airtight container in the refrigerator for up to 3 weeks. Yield: 1-1/2 cups.

Mixed Citrus Marmalade

I have an abundance of grapefruit and oranges, which I put to good use in this tangy, orange-colored marmalade.
—*Corky Huffsmith, Indio, California*

1 pound lemons, thinly sliced and seeds removed
1 pound grapefruit, thinly sliced and seeds removed
1 pound oranges, thinly sliced and seeds removed
2 quarts water
8 cups sugar

1. In a large bowl, combine the lemons, grapefruit, oranges and water. Cover and refrigerate overnight.

2. Transfer to a Dutch oven. Bring to a boil. Reduce heat; simmer, uncovered, for 10-15 minutes or until fruit is tender. Stir in sugar. Bring to a boil. Cook and stir for 45-55 minutes or until thickened, stirring frequently.

3. Remove from the heat; skim off foam. Carefully ladle hot mixture into hot sterilized half-pint jars, leaving 1/4-in. headspace. Remove air bubbles; wipe rims and adjust lids. Process for 5 minutes in a boiling-water canner. **Yield:** 10 half-pints.

Editor's Note: The processing time listed is for altitudes of 1,000 feet or less. Add 1 minute to the processing time for each 1,000 feet of additional altitude.

Herb-Beer Bread Mix

The beer flavor really comes through in this savory loaf. To make a fun Christmas gift, pack a festive basket with a jar of the bread mix as well as the bottle of beer needed to prepare the recipe.
—*Redawna Kalynchuk, Sexsmith, Alberta*

      2-2/3 cups all-purpose flour
          2 tablespoons sugar
          2 teaspoons baking powder
          1 teaspoon salt
          1 teaspoon dried oregano
          1 teaspoon dried thyme
      1/2 teaspoon dill weed
ADDITIONAL INGREDIENTS:
          1 bottle (12 ounces) beer
          1 tablespoon butter, melted

1. In a large bowl, combine the first seven ingredients. Transfer to a 1-qt. glass jar. Cover and store in a cool dry place for up to 6 months. **Yield:** 1 batch (about 3 cups).

2. To prepare bread: Transfer bread mix to a large bowl. Stir in beer just until moistened. Spoon into a greased 9-in. x 5-in. loaf pan. Bake at 375° for 40-45 minutes or until a toothpick inserted near the center comes out clean. Cool for 10 minutes before removing from pan to a wire rack. Brush with butter. **Yield:** 1 loaf (16 slices).

Deb's Cheese Ball

Herbs and walnuts really jazz up this scrumptious spread. Using reduced-fat cheese and mayonnaise makes it a little lighter.
—*Deb Lavengood, New Palestine, Indiana*

          2 packages (8 ounces *each*) reduced-fat
              cream cheese
      1/4 cup reduced-fat mayonnaise
      1/2 cup shredded reduced-fat cheddar cheese
      1/4 cup shredded Parmesan and Romano cheese
          2 teaspoons finely chopped leek (white
              portion only)
      3/4 teaspoon Worcestershire sauce
      1/2 teaspoon garlic powder
      1/2 teaspoon dried chives
      1/2 teaspoon crushed red pepper flakes
      1/4 teaspoon onion powder
      1/4 teaspoon seasoned salt
      1/4 teaspoon dried oregano
          1 teaspoon plus 2 tablespoons minced fresh parsley,
              divided
          2 tablespoons finely chopped walnuts
Assorted crackers

Deb's Cheese Ball

1. In a large bowl, beat cream cheese and mayonnaise until smooth. Stir in the cheeses, leek, Worcestershire sauce, garlic powder, chives, pepper flakes, onion powder, seasoned salt, oregano and 1 teaspoon minced parsley.

2. Cover and refrigerate for at least 1 hour. Shape into a ball and roll in walnuts and remaining parsley; wrap in plastic wrap. Refrigerate for at least 1 hour longer. Serve with crackers. **Yield:** 2-1/2 cups.

Mix for Cranberry Lemonade Bars

I recently put all of our family's treasured recipes into a cookbook so they can be passed down from generation to generation. These cakelike lemon bars came out of that special collection.
—*Suzette Jury, Keene, California*

      2-1/4 cups all-purpose flour
          1 cup sugar
      3/4 teaspoon baking soda
      1/2 teaspoon salt
          1 cup dried cranberries
ADDITIONAL INGREDIENTS:
          1 egg
      1/2 cup butter, softened
      1/3 cup frozen lemonade concentrate, thawed
          1 tablespoon grated lemon peel
Confectioners' sugar

1. In a 1-qt. glass jar, layer the first five ingredients in order listed, packing well between each layer. Cover tightly. Store in a cool dry place for up to 6 months.

2. To prepare bars: In a large bowl, combine the egg, butter, lemonade concentrate, lemon peel and lemon bar mix. Press into a greased 13-in. x 9-in. baking pan. Bake at 350° for 20-25 minutes or until lightly browned. Cool on a wire rack. Dust with confectioners' sugar; cut into bars. **Yield:** 2 dozen.

Tender Sugar Cookies
Scottie Cookies (p. 62)

Mmm! These brightly frosted cutouts, fresh-baked bars, cool meringues and other goodies are perfect for treat trays and gift tins during the Christmas season.

Tender Sugar Cookies

Want to simplify sugar cookies? Roll this buttery dough from our Test Kitchen into balls, then dip them into sugar before baking.

    3/4 cup butter-flavored shortening
  1-1/2 cups sugar
      2 eggs
    1/2 teaspoon almond extract
    1/2 teaspoon vanilla extract
      3 cups all-purpose flour
      1 teaspoon baking powder
      1 teaspoon baking soda
    1/2 teaspoon salt
    1/3 cup buttermilk
  Colored sugar *and/or* coarse sugar

1. In a large bowl, cream shortening and sugar until light and fluffy. Add eggs, one at a time, beating well after each addition. Beat in extracts. Combine the flour, baking powder, baking soda and salt; add to the creamed mixture alternately with buttermilk, beating well after each addition. Cover and refrigerate for at least 2 hours.

2. Roll into 1-in. balls; dip tops in sugar. Place 2 in. apart on parchment paper-lined baking sheets. Bake at 375° for 9-11 minutes or until lightly browned and tops are cracked. Remove to wire racks to cool. Yield: 5-1/2 dozen.

Mint Twist Meringues

I like to sprinkle these light, airy meringues with crushed mints and baking cocoa. —Cheryl Perry, Hertford, North Carolina

      2 egg whites
    1/2 teaspoon cream of tartar
    1/4 teaspoon peppermint extract
    1/3 cup sugar
    1/4 cup crushed red and green mint candies
      1 tablespoon baking cocoa

1. In a large bowl, beat the egg whites, cream of tartar and extract on medium speed until soft peaks form. Gradually beat in sugar, 1 tablespoon at a time, on high until stiff glossy peaks form and sugar is dissolved.

2. Pipe or drop by tablespoonfuls 2 in. apart onto parchment paper-lined baking sheets. Sprinkle with candies.

3. Bake at 325° for 40-45 minutes or until set and dry. Turn the oven off; leave meringues in oven for 1 hour. Remove to wire rack. Sprinkle with cocoa. Store in an airtight container. Yield: 2 dozen.

Turtle Shortbread Cookies

With caramel, chocolate and pecans, these rich wedges taste like turtle candies. —Patricia Schlink, Washington, Illinois

  1-1/2 cups butter, softened
    1/2 cup sugar
      1 teaspoon almond extract
      4 cups all-purpose flour
    1/2 teaspoon salt
     36 caramels
      3 tablespoons 2% milk
  1-1/2 cups chopped pecans
      1 cup (6 ounces) semisweet chocolate chips
      2 teaspoons shortening
     72 pecan halves (about 2 cups)

1. In a large bowl, cream butter, sugar and extract until light and fluffy. Combine flour and salt; gradually add to creamed mixture and mix well.

2. Divide dough into 12 pieces. On a lightly floured surface, roll each portion into a 5-in. circle; cut into six wedges. Place 2 in. apart on greased baking sheets. Bake at 350° for 7-9 minutes or until set. Cool for 2 minutes before removing from pans to wire racks to cool completely.

3. In a microwave, melt caramels with milk; stir until smooth. Dip two edges of each cookie into caramel; allow excess to drip off. Dip edges in chopped pecans. Place on waxed paper.

4. Melt the chocolate chips and shortening; stir until smooth. Spoon about 1/2 teaspoon onto each cookie; immediately top with a pecan half. Let stand until set. Store in an airtight container. Yield: 6 dozen.

Turtle Shortbread Cookies

Cherry Walnut Squares

I call these "naughty but nice" bars! Packed with white chocolate chips, cherries and nuts, they're indulgent and oh-so-good.
— Lisa Speer, Palm Beach, Florida

    3/4 cup butter, softened
    1/3 cup packed brown sugar
      2 tablespoons plus 1-1/2 teaspoons sugar
    1/8 teaspoon almond extract
      2 cups all-purpose flour
    1/8 teaspoon salt
FILLING:
      1 cup plus 2 tablespoons packed brown sugar
    3/4 cup butter, cubed
    1/4 cup light corn syrup
      2 tablespoons heavy whipping cream
    1/4 teaspoon salt
2-3/4 cups chopped walnuts, *divided*
      1 cup dried cherries, chopped
2-1/2 teaspoons vanilla extract
    3/4 cup white baking chips

1. In a large bowl, cream butter, sugars and extract until light and fluffy. Combine flour and salt; gradually add to creamed mixture and mix well. Press onto the bottom of an ungreased 13-in. x 9-in. baking pan. Bake at 375° for 8-10 minutes or until edges begin to brown.

2. Meanwhile, in a large saucepan, combine the brown sugar, butter, corn syrup, whipping cream and salt. Bring to a boil over medium heat, stirring constantly. Reduce heat; cook and stir for 4 minutes or until slightly thickened.

3. Remove from the heat. Stir in 2-1/2 cups walnuts, dried cherries and vanilla; spread over the crust. Bake for 15-20 minutes or until bubbly. Sprinkle with the white baking chips

Cherry Walnut Squares

and remaining walnuts; lightly press into the filling. Cool on a wire rack. Cut into 1-in. squares. **Yield: 6-1/2 dozen.**

Scottie Cookies

(Pictured on page 60)

These decked-out doggy cutouts from our Test Kitchen staff are all bundled up in colorful sweaters for the holiday season.

    1/2 cup butter, softened
    1/2 cup butter-flavored shortening
      2 tablespoons cream cheese, softened
      1 cup sugar
      2 eggs
      1 teaspoon vanilla extract
      1 teaspoon light corn syrup
      4 cups cake flour
      1 teaspoon baking powder
    1/2 teaspoon salt
FROSTING:
      3 cups confectioners' sugar
      3 tablespoons cream cheese, softened
4-1/2 teaspoons light corn syrup
      3 to 4 tablespoons 2% milk
Black liquid food coloring
ROYAL ICING:
      4 cups confectioners' sugar
      6 tablespoons warm water (110° to 115°)
      3 tablespoons meringue powder
Red and green paste food coloring
Assorted sprinkles

1. In a large bowl, cream the butter, shortening, cream cheese and sugar until light and fluffy. Beat in the eggs, vanilla and corn syrup. Combine flour, baking powder and salt; gradually add to creamed mixture and mix well.

2. Divide dough in thirds. Shape each into a ball, then flatten into a disk. Wrap in plastic wrap and refrigerate for 2 hours or until easy to handle.

3. On a lightly floured surface, roll one portion of dough to 1/4-in. thickness. Cut with a floured 3-in. dog-shaped cookie cutter. Place 1 in. apart on parchment paper-lined baking sheets. Repeat with remaining dough.

4. Bake at 375° for 7-9 minutes or until edges are lightly browned. Remove to wire racks to cool completely.

5. For frosting, in a large bowl, combine the confectioners' sugar, cream cheese and corn syrup. Add enough milk to make a thin spreading consistency. Divide in half; tint one half with black food coloring and leave remaining half plain.

6. For royal icing, in a large bowl, combine confectioners' sugar, water and meringue powder; beat on low speed just until combined. Beat on high for 4-5 minutes or until stiff peaks form. Divide in half; tint one portion red and the other green. (Keep unused icing covered at all times with a damp cloth.)

7. Decorate the cookies as desired with frosting, icing and sprinkles. Let dry at room temperature for several hours or until firm. Store in an airtight container in the refrigerator. **Yield: 7 dozen.**

Holiday Fruitcake Cookies

Less sweet and dense than a Christmas fruitcake, these easy drop cookies are guaranteed to please your family and friends.
—Hannah LaRue Rider, East Point, Kentucky

    3/4 cup shortening
      1 cup sugar
      3 eggs
    1/3 cup orange juice
      1 tablespoon rum extract
      3 cups all-purpose flour
      2 teaspoons baking powder
      1 teaspoon baking soda
      1 teaspoon salt
 1-1/2 cups chopped mixed candied fruit
      1 cup raisins
      1 cup chopped pecans

1. In a large bowl, cream shortening and sugar until light and fluffy. Beat in the eggs, orange juice and extract. Combine the flour, baking powder, baking soda and salt; gradually add to creamed mixture and mix well. Stir in the candied fruit, raisins and pecans.

2. Drop by teaspoonfuls 2 in. apart onto ungreased baking sheets. Bake at 350° for 10-12 minutes or until golden brown. Remove to wire racks. Store in an airtight container. Yield: 9 dozen.

Florentines

These Italian cookies feature plenty of almonds and citrus flavor. Melted chocolate and candied cherries make them extra special.
—Cleo Gonske, Redding, California

    3/4 cup sugar
    1/2 cup butter, cubed
    1/4 cup heavy whipping cream
      3 tablespoons honey
      1 teaspoon grated lemon peel
    1/4 teaspoon salt
 1-3/4 cups sliced almonds
      3 tablespoons finely chopped candied
          orange peel
Semisweet chocolate chips, optional
Red *or* green candied cherries, halved, optional

1. In a large saucepan, combine the sugar, butter, cream, honey, lemon peel and salt. Bring to a boil over medium heat, stirring constantly. Reduce heat; cook and stir for 4 minutes or until a candy thermometer reads 225°. Remove from the heat; stir in almonds and orange peel.

2. Drop by scant tablespoonfuls 3 in. apart onto parchment paper-lined baking sheets. Bake at 350° for 6-8 minutes or until golden brown. Immediately flatten warm cookies with the back of a spoon. Cool completely on parchment paper.

3. If desired, melt chips in a microwave; stir until smooth. Spread or brush over bottoms of cookies. Use a fork to create wavy lines in chocolate. Place a cherry half in the center of each. Let stand until set. Yield: 4 dozen.

Gingerbread Cookies with Lemon Frosting

Gingerbread Cookies With Lemon Frosting

When I topped these spicy rounds with my lemony cream-cheese frosting, I knew I had a hit. You'll taste a hint of chai tea, too.
—Aysha Schurman, Ammon, Idaho

    1/2 cup butter, softened
    3/4 cup packed brown sugar
      2 eggs
    1/4 cup molasses
      3 cups all-purpose flour
      1 tablespoon ground ginger
      2 teaspoons baking soda
      1 teaspoon *each* ground cardamom, cinnamon and
          allspice
      1 teaspoon grated lemon peel
    1/2 teaspoon salt
FROSTING:
      4 ounces cream cheese, softened
 2-1/2 cups confectioners' sugar
      2 tablespoons lemon juice
      1 tablespoon grated lemon peel
      1 teaspoon vanilla extract

1. In a large bowl, cream butter and brown sugar until light and fluffy. Beat in the eggs and molasses. Combine the flour, ginger, baking soda, cardamom, cinnamon, allspice, lemon peel and salt; gradually add to creamed mixture and mix well.

2. Shape into 1-in. balls; place 2 in. apart on ungreased baking sheets. Bake at 350° for 8-10 minutes or until tops are cracked. Cool for 2 minutes before removing from pans to wire racks to cool completely.

3. In a small bowl, beat the cream cheese until fluffy. Add the confectioners' sugar, lemon juice, peel and vanilla; beat until smooth. Frost cookies. Store in an airtight container in the refrigerator. Yield: 4 dozen.

Pecan Pinwheels

Pecan Pinwheels

With pecan centers, a pinwheel shape and candied cherries, these festive goodies are a favorite in my house at Christmastime.
—*Lorraine Rothermich, Portage Des Sioux, Missouri*

    1 cup heavy whipping cream
    1 teaspoon white vinegar
    1 package (1/4 ounce) active dry yeast
    2 egg yolks
    2 cups all-purpose flour
  1/2 teaspoon salt
  1/2 cup cold butter
FILLING:
  1/2 cup finely chopped pecans
  1/4 cup plus 2 tablespoons sugar, *divided*
  1/4 cup packed brown sugar
    2 tablespoons 2% milk
   30 candied cherries, halved

1. Place whipping cream in large bowl; let stand out at room temperature for 1 hour. Add vinegar; stir until thickened. Stir in yeast until dissolved; add the egg yolks. In a small bowl, combine flour and salt. Cut in butter. Gradually add to creamed mixture and mix well. Divide dough in half; wrap in plastic wrap. Cover and refrigerate overnight.

2. In a small saucepan, combine pecans, 1/4 cup sugar, brown sugar and milk. Cook and stir over medium heat for 3 minutes; set aside.

3. On a floured surface, roll each portion of cookie dough into a 12-in. x 10-in. rectangle. With a sharp knife or pastry wheel, cut dough into 2-in. squares. Place 3 in. apart on lightly greased baking sheets.

4. Cut through the dough from each corner of the square to within 1/2 in. of the center. Spoon 1/2 teaspoon of filling into the center of each square. Fold alternating points of the square to the center to form a pinwheel. Press a cherry half into the center of each. Sprinkle with remaining sugar.

5. Bake at 350° for 10-12 minutes or until edges begin to brown. Remove to wire racks. Store in an airtight container. **Yield:** 5 dozen.

Cranberry-Pine Nut Shortbread

These rich, buttery shortbread squares are all dressed up for the holiday season with toasted pine nuts and dried cranberries.
—*Joyce Gemperlein, Rockville, Maryland*

  1/2 cup unsalted butter, melted
  1/2 cup confectioners' sugar
  1/4 cup pine nuts, toasted
  1/4 cup dried cranberries, chopped
    1 cup all-purpose flour

1. In a small bowl, combine butter, confectioners' sugar, pine nuts and cranberries. Gradually add flour; mix well (dough will be stiff).

2. Press dough into an ungreased 9-in. square baking pan. Bake at 350° for 18-20 minutes or until edges begin to brown. Cool for 5 minutes; cut into squares. Continue to cool to room temperature. Store in an airtight container. **Yield:** 16 cookies.

Peanut Butter-Filled Cookies

Anyone who likes peanut butter cups is sure to love these treats! For an extra-special finishing touch, place a cake or cookie stencil over the cookies before sprinkling on the confectioners' sugar.
—*Diane Miller, Millersburg, Indiana*

  1/2 cup butter, softened
  1/4 cup peanut butter
  1/2 cup sugar
  1/2 cup packed brown sugar
    1 egg
    1 teaspoon vanilla extract
1-1/4 cups all-purpose flour
  1/2 cup baking cocoa
  1/2 teaspoon baking soda
FILLING:
  3/4 cup confectioners' sugar
  3/4 cup peanut butter
Additional confectioners' sugar

1. In a large bowl, cream butter, peanut butter and sugars until light and fluffy. Beat in egg and vanilla. Combine the flour, cocoa and baking soda; gradually add to the creamed mixture and mix well.

2. In a small bowl, combine confectioners' sugar and peanut butter. Roll into 30 balls. Shape tablespoonfuls of dough around the filling to cover completely; place 2 in. apart on ungreased baking sheets. Flatten with a glass.

3. Bake at 375° for 6-8 minutes or until set. Remove to wire racks. Sprinkle with additional confectioners' sugar. **Yield:** 2-1/2 dozen.

Peanut Butter-Filled Cookies

Gianduja

Candy Confections

Sweeten the holiday season with decadent delights such as Mocha Cream Truffles, Peppermint Swirl Fudge, Irresistible English Toffee and Caramel Nut Logs.

Gianduja

These layered chocolate squares are a bit fancier than my usual lineup of holiday candy, but they're also very popular.
—*Virginia Sauer, Wantagh, New York*

1-1/2 pounds shelled hazelnuts, skins removed
   3/4 cup canola oil
1-1/2 pounds bittersweet chocolate, chopped
   3 milk chocolate Toblerone candy bars (3.52 ounces *each*), chopped

1. Line an 8-in. square dish with foil. Place hazelnuts and oil in a food processor; cover and process until mixture forms a paste.

2. In a large saucepan, melt bittersweet chocolate. Stir in 2-1/4 cups hazelnut mixture. Pour half of mixture into prepared dish. Refrigerate until firm.

3. Melt candy bars; stir in remaining hazelnut mixture. Pour over bittersweet layer. Refrigerate until firm.

4. Reheat remaining bittersweet mixture if necessary; pour over candy bar layer. Refrigerate until firm. Cut into 1-in. squares. Store in an airtight container in the refrigerator. **Yield:** about 3 pounds.

Stained Glass Candy

With a burst of wintergreen flavor, this green-colored hard candy makes a refreshing choice on a Christmas treat tray.
—*Karolin Kershner, Barrington, Illinois*

3-1/2 cups sugar
1-1/2 cups light corn syrup
   1 cup water
   1 tablespoon wintergreen oil
   3 to 4 drops green food coloring

1. Butter a 15-in. x 10-in. x 1-in. pan; set aside.

2. In a large heavy saucepan, combine the sugar, corn syrup and water. Cook and stir over medium heat until the sugar is dissolved. Bring to a boil. Cook, without stirring, until a candy thermometer reads 300° (hard-crack stage).

3. Remove from the heat; stir in oil and food coloring (keep face away from mixture as oil is very strong). Immediately pour into prepared pan; cool. Break into pieces. Store in airtight containers. **Yield:** 2 pounds.

Editor's Note: We recommend that you test your candy thermometer before each use by bringing water to a boil; the thermometer should read 212°. Adjust your recipe temperature up or down based on your test.

Caramel Buckeye Candies

Yum! These rich peanut-butter balls are dipped in caramel, rolled in a crunchy coating and drizzled with melted chocolate.
—*Tiffany Voigt, Hilliard, Ohio*

   3/4 cup creamy peanut butter
   1/4 cup butter, softened
   1/2 teaspoon vanilla extract
1-1/2 cups confectioners' sugar
COATING:
   5 cups crisp rice cereal
1-3/4 cups finely chopped walnuts
   2 packages (14 ounces *each*) caramels
   1 cup butter, cubed
   2 cups white baking chips *and/or* milk chocolate chips

1. In a large bowl, cream the peanut butter and butter until light and fluffy. Beat in vanilla. Gradually add confectioners' sugar until combined. Roll into 1/2-in. balls; place on waxed paper-lined baking sheets. Chill until firm.

2. In a shallow bowl, combine cereal and walnuts; set aside. In a microwave, melt caramels and butter; stir until smooth. Dip balls in caramel; allow excess to drip off. Roll in cereal mixture; return to baking sheets.

3. In a microwave, melt chips; stir until smooth. Drizzle over candies. Refrigerate until set. Store in an airtight container. **Yield:** 5-1/2 dozen.

Caramel Buckeye Candies

Apple Jelly Candy

Soft and fruity, these old-fashioned squares are coated with sugar for a pretty presentation. Walnuts give them a bit of crunch.
—Helen Orestad, Powderville, Montana

    2 cups sugar
1-3/4 cups unsweetened applesauce
    2 envelopes unflavored gelatin
    1 package (3 ounces) lemon gelatin
  1/2 cup chopped walnuts
    1 teaspoon vanilla extract
Superfine, confectioners' *and/or* granulated sugar

1. In a large saucepan, combine the sugar, applesauce and gelatins; let stand for 1 minute. Bring to a boil over medium heat, stirring constantly. Boil for 15 minutes. Remove from the heat; stir in walnuts and vanilla.

2. Immediately pour into a greased 11-in. x 7-in. baking dish. Cover and refrigerate overnight. Cut into 1-in. pieces; roll in superfine, confectioners' and/or granulated sugar. Store in an airtight container in the refrigerator. Yield: about 6 dozen.

Peppermint Swirl Fudge

Indulge in candy-shop flavor with this delectable swirled fudge. For a festive look, I add red food coloring and crushed mints.
—Suzette Jury, Keene, California

    1 teaspoon butter
    1 package (10 to 12 ounces) white baking chips
    1 can (16 ounces) vanilla frosting
  1/2 teaspoon peppermint extract
    8 drops red food coloring
    2 tablespoons crushed peppermint candies

Peppermint Swirl Fudge

1. Line a 9-in. square pan with foil and grease the foil with butter; set aside.

2. In a small saucepan, melt chips; stir until smooth. Remove from the heat. Stir in the frosting and extract. Spread into prepared pan. Randomly place drops of food coloring over fudge; cut through fudge with a knife to swirl. Sprinkle with candies. Refrigerate for 1 hour or until set.

3. Using foil, lift fudge out of pan. Gently peel off foil; cut fudge into 1-in. squares. Store in an airtight container. Yield: about 1-1/2 pounds.

Mocha Cream Truffles

Java lovers just can't get enough of these decadent cookie truffles. Our Test Kitchen experts perked them up by blending in espresso and chocolate-covered coffee beans.

    1 package (18 ounces) cream-filled chocolate
        sandwich cookies
    3 tablespoons instant espresso powder
    1 teaspoon boiling water
    1 package (8 ounces) cream cheese, softened
  1/2 cup chocolate-covered coffee beans, coarsely
        chopped, optional
3-1/2 cups semisweet chocolate chips
    2 tablespoons plus 1-1/2 teaspoons shortening

1. Place cookies in a food processor; cover and process until finely chopped. Dissolve espresso powder in boiling water. Add espresso mixture and cream cheese to cookie crumbs. Cover and process until smooth. Stir in coffee beans if desired.

2. Shape into 1-in. balls. Place on baking sheets; cover and refrigerate for at least 1 hour.

3. In a microwave, melt chocolate chips and shortening; stir until smooth. Dip balls in chocolate, allowing excess to drip off. Place on waxed paper; let stand until set. Store in an airtight container in the refrigerator. Yield: about 4 dozen.

Irresistible English Toffee

The name says it all—this toffee truly is irresistible! A Symphony candy bar and smoked almonds are the secrets to its success.
—Melanie Hanni, Blackfoot, Idaho

    2 teaspoons plus 1 cup butter, *divided*
    1 cup sugar
    2 tablespoons water
    2 tablespoons corn syrup
  1/4 teaspoon salt
    1 can (6 ounces) smoked almonds, chopped
    1 teaspoon vanilla extract
    1 Symphony candy bar with almonds and toffee
        (8 ounces), chopped

1. Grease a 15-in. x 10-in. x 1-in. baking pan with 2 teaspoons butter; set aside.

2. In a small heavy saucepan, combine sugar, water, corn syrup and salt; stir in remaining butter. Cook and stir over medium

heat until a candy thermometer reads 300° (hard-crack stage). Remove from heat; stir in almonds and extract. Immediately pour into prepared pan.

3. Sprinkle with candy bar; spread with a knife when melted. Let stand until set, about 1 hour. Break into pieces. Store in an airtight container. Yield: about 1-1/2 pounds.

Editor's Note: We recommend that you test your candy thermometer before each use by bringing water to a boil; the thermometer should read 212°. Adjust your recipe temperature up or down based on your test.

Grandma's Hazelnut Candies

Making these yummy bites requires just three basic ingredients—white baking chips, hazelnut spread and toasted nuts.
—Sharon Tipton, Winter Garden, Florida

    1 package (10 to 12 ounces) white baking chips
    3/4 cup chocolate hazelnut spread
1-1/2 cups chopped hazelnuts, toasted, *divided*

1. In a small saucepan, combine baking chips and hazelnut spread; cook and stir over low heat until smooth. Remove from the heat. Stir in 1 cup hazelnuts.

2. Drop by tablespoonfuls onto waxed paper-lined baking sheets; sprinkle with remaining nuts. Refrigerate until firm. Store in an airtight container. Yield: about 4-1/2 dozen.

Editor's Note: Look for chocolate hazelnut spread in the peanut butter section.

Caramel Nut Logs

These wrapped caramel logs rolled in peanuts never stick around long. It's a good thing the recipe makes a big batch!
—Karen Haen, Sturgeon Bay, Wisconsin

    4 cups (1-1/3 pounds) chopped salted peanuts,
        divided
    3 cups sugar, *divided*
1-1/3 cups light corn syrup, *divided*
    1 cup water, *divided*
    2 egg whites
  1/4 cup butter, melted
    2 teaspoons vanilla extract
  1/8 teaspoon salt
COATING:
    2 cups sugar
1-1/2 cups half-and-half cream, *divided*
1-1/4 cups light corn syrup
    1 teaspoon vanilla extract
  1/4 teaspoon salt
Additional chopped salted peanuts

1. Line a 15-in. x 10-in. x 1-in. baking pan with foil; spray foil with cooking spray. Sprinkle with 2 cups peanuts; set aside.

2. In a small heavy saucepan, combine 3/4 cup sugar, 2/3 cup corn syrup and 1/4 cup water. Bring to a boil over medium heat, stirring constantly. Reduce the heat to medium-low.

Caramel Nut Logs

Cook, without stirring, until a candy thermometer reads 250° (hard-ball stage).

3. Meanwhile, beat the egg whites in a heat-proof large bowl until stiff peaks form. With mixer running on high speed, carefully add the hot syrup in a slow steady stream, beating constantly at high speed for 5 minutes or until thickened. Cover and set aside.

4. In a large heavy saucepan, combine remaining sugar, corn syrup and water. Bring to a boil over medium heat, stirring constantly. Reduce heat to medium-low; cook, without stirring, until a candy thermometer reads 290° (soft-crack stage).

5. Gradually pour hot syrup into egg white mixture; stir with a wooden spoon. Stir in the butter, vanilla and salt.

6. Pour mixture over peanuts in pan; press down evenly with buttered fingers.

7. For the coating, in a large saucepan, combine the sugar, 1/2 cup cream and corn syrup. Bring to a boil over medium heat, stirring constantly; add remaining cream. Reduce heat to medium-low; cook and stir until a candy thermometer reads 242° (soft-ball stage).

8. Remove from the heat; stir in the vanilla and salt. Pour over nougat layer in pan. Sprinkle with remaining peanuts, pressing slightly into nougat. Cool for at least 2 hours or until set. Cut into 1-1/2 in. x 1-in. pieces. Roll edges in additional peanuts and shape into logs. Wrap in waxed paper. Store at room temperature. Yield: 4-1/2 pounds.

Editor's Note: We recommend that you test your candy thermometer before each use by bringing water to a boil; the thermometer should read 212°. Adjust your recipe temperature up or down based on your test.

Get Christmas Kicks With a
Sweet Stocking

STARTING OFF the holiday season on the right foot is easy when you prepare an extra-special treat. Created in our Test Kitchen, this cute-as-can-be dessert makes a merry centerpiece as well as a sweet finale to December feasts.

Our cooks cut the stocking out of a homemade sheet cake (see the pattern on page 112). With tinted buttercream frosting and colored sugar, they made the plain stocking a festive red color and added a fluffy white cuff.

For even more fun, Christmas cookies and candies stacked at the top of the cuff give the stocking a "stuffed" look. They serve as additional goodies for guests, too.

So why not make a yummy cake of your own? Your stockings on the mantel won't be the only ones brimming with cheer!

Stocking Cake

Pattern on page 112
2-1/4 cups butter, softened
    12 ounces cream cheese, softened
4-1/2 cups sugar
    12 eggs
1-1/2 teaspoons vanilla extract
4-1/2 cups cake flour
FROSTING:
    1/2 cup all-purpose flour
1-1/2 cups 2% milk
1-1/2 cups butter, softened
1-1/2 cups sugar
1-1/2 teaspoons vanilla extract
Red paste food coloring
FINISHING TOUCHES:
Red colored sugar
White edible glitter
Assorted cookies and candies

Line a greased and floured 18-in. x 12-in. baking pan with waxed paper; grease and flour the paper. Set aside.

In a large bowl, cream the butter, cream cheese and sugar until light and fluffy. Add eggs, one at a time, beating well after each addition. Beat in vanilla. Add flour; mix well. Pour into prepared pan.

Bake at 325° for 40-45 minutes or until a toothpick inserted near the center comes out clean. Cool for 10 minutes before removing from pan to a wire rack to cool completely.

Meanwhile, in a small saucepan, whisk flour and milk until smooth. Bring to a boil; cook and stir for 2 minutes or until thickened. Cover; cool to room temperature.

Trace the enlarged pattern onto waxed paper; cut out. Place pattern over cake; with a sharp knife, cut out. Discard the scraps or save for another use. Transfer cake to a covered cake board.

In a small bowl, cream the butter and sugar until light and fluffy. Beat in vanilla. Add the milk mixture; beat for 10 minutes or until fluffy.

Tint 2-1/2 cups frosting red; spread 1-1/2 cups red frosting over the stocking portion of cake. Coat the sides and top of the stocking with red sugar. Spread or pipe white frosting over the cuff; pipe the remaining red frosting around edge of stocking. Sprinkle the cuff with white edible glitter.

Fill stocking with cookies and candies. **Yield:** 14 servings.

Tips!

When Making the Stocking Cake

- Grab a few goodies from your Christmas cookie tray to decorate the area above the cuff of the cake. Or, use prepared cookies and candies from a bakery, grocery store or confectionery. On the cake shown in the photo at far left, our cooks included one of the cute Scottie Cookies from this book (recipe on page 62).

- If you like, use fewer cookies and candies at the top of the cake and prop them up using frosted cupcakes—or scraps of cake left over after cutting out the stocking.

- To create the same fluffy stocking cuff our cooks did, fill a gallon-size plastic storage bag with frosting, press out the excess air and seal the bag. Push the frosting down to one corner and pinch the corner flat. With scissors, snip off a 3/4-inch corner. Pipe generous squiggles, moving in rows, from one side of the cuff to the other.

- It's easier to achieve the bright red color of frosting shown in the photo if you tint the frosting with pink food coloring before the red food coloring. Sprinkle the frosted stocking with red sugar to make the color even more vibrant.

- To give the cake a finished look, our cooks added a shell border around the red area of the stocking. You can do the same using either an open or closed star pastry tip. For even more detail, pipe stitching on the heel and toe sections of the stocking using additional red (or black) frosting.

A Winter Show

Jean Vasecka, Uniontown, Pennsylvania

Winter winds are whistling through the trees around my home
Across the yard go tiny tracks where rabbits dare to roam

The houses hung from frosty limbs are occupied by squirrels
They watch as flakes come falling down in graceful little swirls

Atop the feeder on a branch, a bird has stopped to eat
It shivers in the wintry cold while savoring its treat

And all of them are unaware they're putting on a show
I watch them from my window seat, protected from the snow!

Christmas Eve

Dale Graumann, Winnipeg, Manitoba

A frosty night, a home so warm
With loved ones gathered near
Christmas everywhere we look
And spirits full of cheer

Mom is baking one last time
The tree is trimmed and bright
Father tells us all the tale
Of Jesus born this night.

It's love that makes us gather here
Not presents from a store
Our family, both young and old
Together one time more

Loving hearts for all we see
Will make this Christmas right
Just like the first one, long ago
On yet another night.

BRING SUGAR AND SPICE to the season by hosting a ladies' tea party steeped in Victorian style. It's a wonderful way to reconnect with friends and treat them to some holiday cheer.

Set the scene in your home by using your prettiest dishes and dainty decorations to create the look of a Victorian parlor. You'll pour on even more charm when you serve trays of teas, scones, finger sandwiches and other delicacies (see the menu below and the recipes on pages 76-78).

Turn to page 79 for additional ideas, from fancy table favors and decorations to fashionable ways of dressing up for the occasion. Your tea party is sure to be spot-on!

Party Menu

Pear-Walnut Tea Sandwiches
Ginger Loaf with Apricot-Ricotta Spread

Ginger Loaf with Apricot-Ricotta Spread

—Joyce Brantl, Victor, New York

   1/4 cup butter, softened
   3/4 cup sugar
   1/4 cup molasses
     1 egg
     2 cups all-purpose flour
     1 teaspoon ground ginger
     1 teaspoon salt
   3/4 teaspoon baking soda
   3/4 teaspoon ground cinnamon
   1/4 teaspoon ground cloves
   3/4 cup 2% milk
SPREAD:
     1 cup ricotta cheese
   1/2 cup finely chopped dried apricots
   1/4 cup confectioners' sugar
     1 teaspoon grated orange peel

1. In a large bowl, cream the butter, sugar and molasses until light and fluffy. Add egg; beat well. Combine flour, ginger, salt, baking soda, cinnamon and cloves; add to the creamed mixture alternately with the milk, beating well after each addition.

2. Transfer to a greased and floured 9-in. x 5-in. loaf pan. Bake at 350° for 40-45 minutes or until a toothpick inserted near the center comes out clean. Cool for 10 minutes before removing from pan to a wire rack to cool completely.

3. In a small bowl, combine the ricotta cheese, dried apricots, confectioners' sugar and orange peel.

4. Cut the edges off the cooled loaf and cut into 16 slices. Spread 2 tablespoons prepared spread over each of eight bread slices; top with remaining bread. Cut each sandwich into four 1-in.-wide strips. **Yield:** 32 tea sandwiches.

Pear-Walnut Tea Sandwiches

—David Bostedt, Zephyrhills, Florida

   1/2 cup mayonnaise
   1/3 cup chopped peeled ripe pears
     2 tablespoons minced fresh tarragon
     2 tablespoons chopped walnuts, toasted
     1 teaspoon Dijon mustard
   1/4 teaspoon salt
   1/8 teaspoon pepper
   16 thin slices white *or* pumpernickel bread, crusts removed
   16 slices deli chicken
     2 cups fresh arugula

In a small bowl, combine the first seven ingredients; spread on one side of each bread slice. Layer half of the slices with chicken and arugula. Top with remaining bread. Cut each sandwich in half diagonally or cut each with a 3-in. round cookie cutter. **Yield:** 16 tea sandwiches (cut in half) or 8 tea sandwiches (cut with cookie cutter).

Rosemary-Lemon Scones

—David Byland, Shawnee, Oklahoma

    2 cups all-purpose flour
    3 tablespoons sugar
    2 teaspoons baking powder
    1/2 teaspoon baking soda
    1/2 teaspoon salt
    5 tablespoons cold butter
    1 cup (8 ounces) sour cream
    1 egg
    2 teaspoons grated lemon peel
    1 teaspoon minced fresh rosemary
    1 teaspoon coarse sugar

1. In a large bowl, combine the flour, sugar, baking powder, baking soda and salt. Cut in butter until mixture resembles coarse crumbs. Whisk sour cream and egg; stir into crumb mixture just until moistened. Stir in lemon peel and rosemary. Turn onto a floured surface; knead 10 times.

2. Pat into an 8-in. circle. Cut into eight wedges, but do not separate. Place on an ungreased baking sheet. Sprinkle with coarse sugar. Bake at 400° for 15-18 minutes or until golden brown. Serve warm. Yield: 8 scones.

Almond Cream Spritz

Almond Cream Spritz

—Jo-Anne Cooper, Camrose, Alberta

    1 cup butter, softened
    1 package (3 ounces) cream cheese, softened
    1/2 cup sugar
    1/2 teaspoon almond extract
    1/4 teaspoon vanilla extract
    2 cups all-purpose flour
    1/2 cup finely chopped almonds

1. In a large bowl, cream the butter, cream cheese and sugar until light and fluffy. Beat in extracts. Gradually add flour. Cover and refrigerate for 30 minutes.

2. Using a cookie press fitted with the disk of your choice, press dough 2 in. apart onto ungreased baking sheets. Sprinkle with almonds. Bake at 375° for 8-10 minutes or until set. Cool for 1 minute before removing from pans to wire racks. Store in an airtight container. Yield: 3 dozen.

Merry Christmas Tea

(Pictured on page 79)

—Taste of Home Test Kitchen

    1/3 cup minced fresh gingerroot
    2 cinnamon sticks (3 inches), crushed
    8 cups pomegranate juice
    2 cups water
    12 individual Raspberry Zinger tea bags
    1/3 cup honey

1. Place ginger and cinnamon sticks on a double thickness of cheesecloth. Bring up corners of cloth; tie with a string to form a bag. Set aside.

2. Place juice and water in a large saucepan. Bring to a boil. Remove from the heat. Add tea bags and spice bag; cover and steep for 8 minutes. Discard tea bags and spice bag; stir in honey. Serve warm. Yield: 9 servings (2-1/4 quarts).

Rosemary-Lemon Scones

Holiday English Trifles

Citrus Tea with Tarragon
—Mary Walters, Westerville, Ohio

　1/2 cup sugar
　1/2 cup orange juice
　1/4 cup plus 8 cups water, *divided*
　1/4 cup honey
　　3 tablespoons lemon juice
　　2 tablespoons lime juice
　1/2 cup fresh tarragon leaves
　　4 individual Earl Grey tea bags
OPTIONAL SUGARED RIM:
　1/2 cup coarse sugar
　　1 teaspoon minced fresh tarragon
　　1 teaspoon grated orange peel
Orange wedges

1. In a small saucepan, combine sugar, orange juice, 1/4 cup water, honey and lemon and lime juices. Bring to a boil over medium-high heat, stirring constantly. Remove from the heat. Let stand for 15 minutes. Transfer to a blender. Add tarragon leaves; cover and process for 30 seconds or until blended. Strain and set aside.

2. In a large saucepan, bring the remaining water to a boil. Remove from the heat; add tea bags. Cover and steep for 3-5 minutes. Discard tea bags. Stir in citrus mixture.

3. If a sugared rim is desired, sprinkle the sugar, tarragon and orange peel on a plate. Using orange wedges, moisten the rims of eight mugs; hold the mugs upside down and dip the rim into the sugar mixture. Serve warm tea in mugs. **Yield:** 8 servings (2 quarts).

Holiday English Trifles
—Bonnie Cameron, Colbert, Washington

　　1 package (18-1/4 ounces) yellow cake mix
　1/3 cup orange juice *or* orange liqueur
　1/3 cup sherry *or* additional orange juice
　　1 jar (18 ounces) seedless raspberry jam
1-1/2 cups cold 2% milk
　　1 package (3.4 ounces) instant vanilla pudding mix
　　1 cup (8 ounces) reduced-fat sour cream
　　2 cups heavy whipping cream
　　3 tablespoons confectioners' sugar
1-1/2 cups fresh raspberries

1. Prepare and bake cake according to package directions, using a greased 13-in. x 9-in baking pan. Cool; cut cake into 1-in. cubes.

2. In a small bowl combine orange juice and sherry. In another bowl, whisk jam. In a large bowl, whisk milk and pudding mix for 2 minutes. Whisk in sour cream. Let stand for 2 minutes or until soft-set.

3. Divide half of the cake cubes among 15 parfait glasses or dessert dishes; drizzle with half of the juice mixture. Layer each with jam and pudding mixture. Top with the remaining cake cubes; drizzle with the remaining juice mixture. Cover and refrigerate for at least 4 hours or overnight.

4. Just before serving, in a large bowl, beat whipping cream until it begins to thicken. Add confectioners' sugar; beat until stiff peaks form. Dollop over the trifles and garnish with fresh raspberries. **Yield:** 15 servings.

Citrus Tea with Tarragon

Merry Christmas Tea

more ideas for a VICTORIAN *tea party*

- Want additional options for your menu? Consider Spiced Apricot Tea (page 26), Mocha Chip Hazelnut Scones (page 36), Turtle Shortbread Cookies (page 61), Gingerbread Cookies with Lemon Frosting (page 63), Holiday Fruitcake Cookies (page 63) and Cranberry-Pine Nut Shortbread (page 64).

- Enhance your teas by offering add-ins— lump sugar, milk, honey and slices of lemon. Serving scones? Present spreads such as whipped butter, preserves, jam, jelly, marmalade, Devonshire cream or lemon curd.

- Fun favors always send off guests with a smile. Surprise them with English party crackers, teacup candles or lacy hand fans. Or, bake an extra batch of yummy Almond Cream Spritz (page 77) or one of the other cookies listed above and pack them into take-home bags.

- On your invitations, encourage guests to get in the spirit of the occasion with their wardrobe. Invite them to dress in Victorian-style clothing or to wear an accessory such as elegant gloves, a piece of cameo jewelry, a string of pearls or an elaborate hat.

- Choose romantic, feminine decorations like fancy dishes, pretty ribbons, beads, doilies, feathers, lace, candles, flowers, embroidery and tassels. For a seasonal touch, display Victorian-style Christmas cards and evergreen wreaths. Focus on the popular colors of the era—burgundy, red, dark green, gold, pink and cream.

Seasonal
CRAFTS

Get creative this Christmas by making any of the heartwarming gifts and decorations here.

Count on Fun With Trio of Felt Trims

THREE is anything but a crowd when it comes to these adorable ornaments. In Conrad, Montana, Renee Dent gave the stitched snowman a pocket—great for a gift card or other small present.

MATERIALS NEEDED:
(For all):
Patterns on page 82
Tracing paper and pencil
Scissors
Tapestry needle
Tacky craft glue
Red string for hanging loops
Ruler
(For candy cane):
Felt—9-inch x 12-inch piece or scraps each of white and red
Red six-strand embroidery floss
5-inch length of 1/8-inch-wide green satin ribbon
(For snowman):
Felt—9-inch x 12-inch piece or scraps each of white, green, dark brown, orange and black
Six-strand embroidery floss—white, black, green, mahogany and orange
3/8-inch red button
7-inch length of 1/8-inch-wide green satin ribbon
(For hobby horse):
Felt—9-inch x 12-inch piece or scraps each of red, green, dark brown and cream
Six-strand embroidery floss—red, dark brown, dark yellow and cream
1/8-inch-wide red satin ribbon—3-inch length and 5-inch length

FINISHED SIZE: Excluding hanging loops, snowman ornament is about 4 inches wide x 3-1/2 inches high, candy cane ornament is about 2 inches wide x 4-1/2 inches high and hobby horse ornament is about 5 inches wide x 4-1/2 inches high.

DIRECTIONS:
Refer to the photo at left as a guide while creating ornaments as directed in the instructions that follow.

Use tapestry needle for all stitching. Separate six-strand embroidery floss and use two strands for all stitching.

CANDY CANE: Trace candy cane pattern onto tracing paper with pencil and cut out.

Cut two candy canes from white felt and cut one from red felt. Cut red candy cane into sections, creating stripes to be added to one white candy cane.

Arrange red stripes on one white candy cane with outer edges matching. Using red floss, blanket-stitch only the interior edges of each stripe to secure in place. See Fig. 1 at far right for stitch illustration.

Place striped candy cane right side up on top of remaining white candy cane with edges matching. Using red floss, blanket-stitch around both candy canes to join them.

Tie ribbon in a bow and glue to candy cane. Let dry.

Cut desired length of red string. Using tapestry needle, attach string to top center of candy cane. Tie ends in a knot to form a hanging loop.

SNOWMAN: Trace snowman head, hat, eye, nose and holly leaf patterns separately onto tracing paper with pencil and cut out.

From white felt, cut two snowman heads. From green felt, cut one holly leaf. From dark brown felt, cut two snowman hats. From orange felt, cut one snowman nose. From black felt, cut two snowman eyes.

Using black floss, blanket-stitch eyes onto one snowman head. Using orange floss, blanket-stitch nose below eyes. Using black floss, make a running stitch to form mouth. See Fig. 2 for stitch illustration.

Place stitched head right side up onto remaining head with edges matching. Using white floss and leaving the straight edge unstitched, blanket-stitch around the curved edge to join head pieces.

With hat edges matching, place one hat over top front of snowman and place remaining hat over top back of snowman.

Use mahogany floss to blanket-stitch along sides of hat, joining the sides and leaving the top and bottom edges of hat unstitched.

Without stitching all the way through snowman, use mahogany floss to blanket-stitch the top and bottom edges of each hat piece separately, creating a pocket opening in ornament.

Glue ribbon just above hat brim, overlapping ribbon ends in back. Let dry.

Using green floss, blanket-stitch around holly leaf. In same way, make a running stitch down center of leaf to form vein. Glue leaf to hat. Let dry.

Using green floss, sew button to base of leaf.

Cut desired length of red string. Using tapestry needle, attach string to top center of hat back only. Tie ends in a knot to form a hanging loop.

HOBBY HORSE: Trace hobby horse body, mane, saddle and rocker patterns separately onto tracing paper with pencil and cut out.

From red felt, cut two rockers. From green felt, cut one saddle. From dark brown felt, cut one mane, clipping into one long edge of the piece as shown in photo to form fringe. From cream felt, cut two bodies.

Use red floss to blanket-stitch the curved edge of saddle onto one body, leaving top straight edge unstitched.

Using dark brown floss, make a running stitch to form the nose, ears and eyelashes. In same way, make a French knot for the eye. See Fig. 3 for stitch illustration.

Fig. 1 Blanket stitch

Fig. 2 Running stitch

Fig. 3 French knot

Fig. 4 Smyrna cross

(Continued on next page)

Cut six 3-1/2-inch pieces of dark brown floss and stack together with ends even. Cut one 4-inch piece of same floss and tie around center of stacked pieces. Tie a knot in the 4-inch piece to secure stacked pieces in place. Fold in half to form tail. Set aside.

Place stitched body right side up on remaining body with the edges matching. Use red floss to blanket-stitch the top straight edge of the saddle, joining the body pieces.

Insert mane between body pieces with fringe of mane out. Use cream floss to blanket-stitch the front and back body pieces separately along the mane, attaching mane to body.

Insert folded tail between body pieces with cut ends of tail out. Use cream floss to blanket-stitch around all unstitched edges of body pieces to join them, stitching over tail to secure in place.

Using dark yellow floss, make a Smyrna cross on each end of one rocker. See Fig. 4 for stitch illustration.

With rocker edges matching, place stitched rocker over bottom front of legs and place remaining rocker over bottom back of legs. Use red floss to blanket-stitch around edges to join rockers, attaching them to legs.

Glue 3-inch ribbon around horse between nose and eye, overlapping ribbon ends in back. Let dry.

Tie 5-inch ribbon in a bow and glue to saddle. Let dry.

Cut desired length of red string. Using tapestry needle, attach string to the base of the mane. Tie the ends in a knot to form a hanging loop. ❋

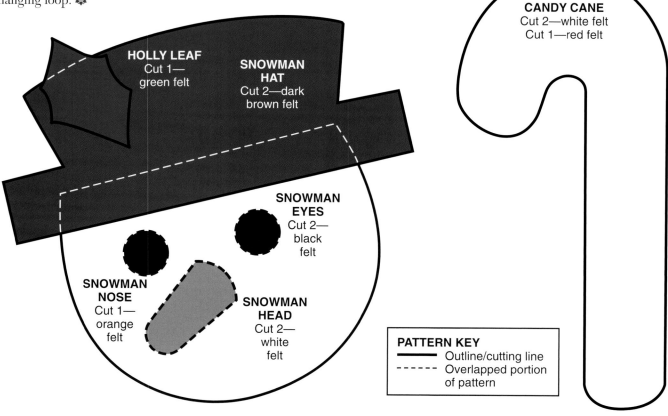

ORNAMENT PATTERNS
Trace 1 each—tracing paper

HOBBY HORSE MANE
Cut 1—dark brown felt

Place mane here

HOBBY HORSE SADDLE
Cut 1—green felt

Place tail here

HOBBY HORSE BODY
Cut 2—cream felt

HOBBY HORSE ROCKER
Cut 2—red felt

CANDY CANE
Cut 2—white felt
Cut 1—red felt

HOLLY LEAF
Cut 1—green felt

SNOWMAN HAT
Cut 2—dark brown felt

SNOWMAN EYES
Cut 2—black felt

SNOWMAN NOSE
Cut 1—orange felt

SNOWMAN HEAD
Cut 2—white felt

PATTERN KEY
——— Outline/cutting line
- - - - Overlapped portion of pattern

Small Santa Cap Is Tops on Trees

HATS OFF to this crocheted design from Donna Collinsworth, of Lewis Center, Ohio. She used red and white yarn to stitch a miniature Santa Claus hat for a cute-as-can-be ornament.

MATERIALS NEEDED:
Worsted-weight yarn—2 ounces each of white and red
Size H/8 (5mm) crochet hook
Yarn or tapestry needle
2-inch-long piece of cardboard
Scissors

FINISHED SIZE: Excluding the tassel, hat ornament is about 4 inches high x 5 inches wide.

DIRECTIONS:
HAT: With red yarn, ch 27, join with sl st in first ch to form a ring.

Round 1: Ch 1, hdc in each st around, sl st top beginning hdc, ch 1, turn (27 sts).

Rounds 2-3: Hdc in each st around, sl st top beginning hdc, ch 1, turn.

Round 4: [Hdc2tog, hdc next 7 sts] around, sl st top beginning hdc, ch 1, turn (24 sts).

Round 5: [Hdc2tog, hdc next 6 sts] around, sl st top beginning hdc, ch 1, turn (21 sts).

Round 6: [Hdc2tog, hdc next 5 sts] around, sl st top beginning hdc, ch 1, turn (18 sts).

Rounds 7-9: Hdc in each st around, sl st top beginning hdc, ch 1, turn.

Round 10: [Hdc2tog, hdc next 4 sts] around, sl st top beginning hdc, ch 1, turn (15 sts).

Round 11: Hdc in each st around, sl st top beginning hdc, ch 1, turn.

Round 12: [Hdc2tog, hdc next 3 sts] around, sl st top beginning hdc, ch 1, turn (12 sts).

Round 13: Hdc in each st around, sl st top beginning hdc, ch 1, turn.

Round 14: [Hdc2tog, hdc next 2 sts] around, sl st top beginning hdc, ch 1, turn (9 sts).

Rounds 15-16: Hdc in each st around, sl st top beginning hdc, ch 1, turn.

Round 17: [Hdc2tog, hdc next st] around, sl st top beginning hdc, ch 1, turn (6 sts).

Round 18: Hdc in each st around, sl st top beginning hdc, ch 1, turn.

Round 19: [Hdc2tog] around, sl st top beginning hdc, fasten off (3 sts).

TRIM: Row 1: With white yarn, ch 3, sc 2nd ch from hk, sc last ch, turn (2 sts).

Row 2: [Ch 4, sl st next st] across, ch 1, turn (forms 2 loops).

Row 3: Press loops to back of piece, sc each st across, turn (2 sts).

Rows 4-59: Repeat Rows 2-3. End Row 59 and fasten off.

With needle and white yarn, sew trim to bottom of hat. Fold top of hat over so the tip is even with the hat's bottom edge. Using red yarn, stitch folded hat in place.

TASSEL: Wrap white yarn around the 2-inch length of the cardboard piece 25 times. Cut a 6-inch piece of white yarn. Slide the wrapped yarn off the cardboard and insert the 6-inch piece of yarn through the center loops. Tie a knot at the top in the center of the 6-inch piece of yarn to hold all yarn loops in place.

Cut a 10-inch piece of white yarn. Wrap piece a few times around the outside of the yarn loops about 1/2 inch down from the top. Tie a knot and trim ends. Cut through all of the loops at the bottom. Trim ends evenly. Tie tassel to the top pointed end of hat.

HANGING LOOP: Cut a 6-inch length of red yarn. Insert one end into center stitches on top fold of hat. Pull yarn through halfway. Tie ends in a knot to form a loop. ❀

ABBREVIATIONS			
ch(s)	chain(s)	hk	hook
sc(s)	single crochet(s)	sl st	slip stitch
hdc(s)	half double crochet(s)	st(s)	stitch(es)
hdc2tog	half double crochet two together (decrease)		

[ ] Instructions between brackets are repeated as directed.

Wood Letters Spell Out Seasonal Cheer

SPREAD THE WORD about your Christmas spirit with this "Merry" accent. In Petaluma, California, Loretta Mateik painted precut wood letters and attached blocks on back to stand them up. If you like, spell "Joy," "Noel" or another seasonal message.

MATERIALS NEEDED:
Desired wood letters spelling "MERRY" (Loretta used letters measuring about 6 inches high x 4 inches wide x 1/4 inch thick)
Nine 3/4-inch wood blocks
1/2-inch checker stencil
Small stencil brush
Paintbrushes—large flat and liner
Paper towels
Water basin
Palette or foam plate
Acrylic craft paints—red, green and black
Finishing sandpaper and tack cloth
Tacky craft glue or wood glue

EDITOR'S NOTE: If necessary, use a scroll saw to trim off the bottom of each wood letter to create a flat standing edge before beginning this project.

FINISHED SIZE: Including attached block base, each letter shown is approximately 6 inches high x 4 inches wide x 1 inch thick.

DIRECTIONS:
Refer to the photo above as a guide while creating the letters as directed in the instructions that follow.

Using sandpaper, sand wood letters until smooth. Wipe with tack cloth to remove sanding dust.

PAINTING: Keep paper towels and a container of water handy to clean paintbrushes. Place dabs of each paint color onto the palette or foam plate as needed. Add coats of paint as needed for complete coverage, letting paint dry after each application.

Using red paint and the large flat paintbrush, paint the M, one R, the Y and five wood blocks.

Using green paint and the large flat paintbrush, paint the E, the remaining R and four wood blocks.

Using black paint, checker stencil and stencil brush, paint checks on the bottom front of the red letters.

Use black paint and the liner to paint an outline around the edge on front of all letters, ending the outline just above the checks on the red letters.

Using red paint and the liner, paint clusters of dots in random areas just inside the black outline on the green letters.

FINISHING: Glue two red wood blocks to the bottom back side of the M and red R, lining up the bottoms of the blocks and letters so that the letters will stand securely. In same way, glue one red wood block to the bottom back side of the Y.

In same way, glue two green blocks to the bottom back side of each green letter.

Let letters dry completely. ✿

Style Blooms in Flowery Necklace

FASHION some fun for the holidays with this unique necklace from Sarah Farley, of Menomonee Falls, Wisconsin. She accented it with a handmade fabric flower and coordinating ribbon.

MATERIALS NEEDED:
Patterns on this page
Tracing paper and pencil
Three large jump rings
Small jump ring
Closing clasp
10mm dark gray glass pearl
Two 20-inch lengths of 3/8-inch gray sheer ribbon
7-3/4-inch length of chunky chain
Variety of small silver chain styles in the following
    lengths—9 inches, 9-1/2 inches, 9-3/4 inches,
    10-1/2 inches and 14 inches
Variety of small black chain styles in the following
    lengths—9 inches, 9-1/4 inches, 9-3/4 inches and
    14 inches
1/8 yard or scraps each of gray tulle and gray 100%
    polyester fabric
Liquid Stitch adhesive
Needle-nose pliers
Scissors
12-inch length of black all-purpose thread
Sewing needle

FINISHED SIZE: Flower necklace measures 24 inches in circumference.

DIRECTIONS:
Refer to the photo below right as a guide while making necklace as directed in the instructions that follow.

FLOWER: Trace patterns separately onto tracing paper with pencil and cut out. From both fabric and tulle, cut five large petals and five small petals.

Glue the narrow base of one large tulle petal directly on top of the narrow base of one large fabric petal. Let dry. Repeat four more times with remaining large tulle and large fabric petals, creating a total of five sets of glued large petals.

Repeat with the small tulle and small fabric petals, creating five sets of glued small petals.

Cut a 1/4-inch slit into the bottom narrow edge of one glued petal set. Put a small dab of glue on one side of the slit, then pull the other side on top of the glued side, making the petal bend upward slightly. Gently press in place and let dry.

In same way, shape all remaining petal sets.

Put a small dab of glue on the narrow base of one large petal. Overlap the glued base with another large petal base, positioning the top petal at a slight angle.

Continue gluing large petals on top of the glued petals in the same way until all large petals are glued in a circle shape, resembling a flower. Let dry.

In same way, glue together all small petals to form a circle shape for flower. Let dry.

Put a dab of glue on the back of the small petal circle. Place in the center of large petal circle. Let dry. Set flower aside.

NECKLACE: Using pliers, slightly open two large jump rings by pulling front to back rather than to the side. Excluding the 14-inch chains, attach one end of each of the small silver chains and small black chains to a jump ring. Attach the opposite end of the chains to remaining open jump ring, leaving the jump rings open for now.

Place one end of the chunky chain on one of the open jump rings. Close that jump ring only. On opposite end of chunky chain, attach the small jump ring and the closing clasp.

Holding the two ribbons together with edges even, thread ribbons through the remaining large open jump ring. Fold ribbons in half so jump ring is in center of ribbons. Attach one end of each 14-inch chain to jump ring, then close ring.

Thread needle with 12-inch length of thread and knot the end. Place the flower over the large jump ring at the folded ribbon base. Bring the needle from back to front through all layers of ribbon next to the jump ring and then through the flower, allowing the knot to get caught in the ribbon. Thread on the pearl. Push needle back through flower and ribbon. Secure in place with a knot on back side of flower and ribbon.

Holding the ribbon pieces together as one piece, braid the two loose 14-inch chains with the ribbons. At the end, attach the chains to the remaining large jump ring. Tie the ribbon ends in a knot around the jump ring. Dab glue on the knot to secure it and let dry.

Trim excess ribbon. Attach clasp to large jump ring to close necklace for wearing. ✿

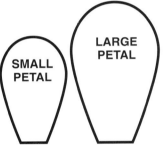

NECKLACE PATTERNS
Trace 1 each—tracing paper
Cut 5 each—polyester fabric
Cut 5 each—tulle

SMALL PETAL

LARGE PETAL

Dressed-Up Bird Delivers Greetings

JUST WING IT this holiday season with handcrafted cards for everyone on your list. This colorful penguin from Sandy Rollinger, of Apollo, Pennsylvania, is sure to make loved ones smile.

MATERIALS NEEDED:
Patterns on this page
Tracing paper and pencil
5-inch x 7-inch white card with envelope
Card stock—scraps of black, white, green, blue and orange
One sheet or scrap of coordinating snowflake-patterned scrapbook paper
Two small wiggle eyes
Craft glue for paper
Powdered cosmetic blush
Cotton swab
1/2-inch snowflake paper punch
Paper crimper
Compass
Ruler
Black fine-line marker
Scissors
Computer and printer (optional)

FINISHED SIZE: Card is 7 inches high x 5 inches wide.

DIRECTIONS:
Refer to the photo above as a guide while assembling the card as directed in the instructions that follow.

Cut a 4-3/4-inch x 6-3/4-inch piece of snowflake paper. Glue snowflake piece centered onto card front.

From green card stock, cut two 3/4-inch x 5-inch and two 3/4-inch x 7-inch rectangles. Run each piece through paper crimper. Glue short pieces to the top and bottom edges of card front, then glue long pieces to side edges of card front.

Trace patterns separately onto tracing paper with pencil and cut out patterns. From blue card stock, cut one hat top, two scarf ends and one 7/8-inch x 2-3/4-inch rectangle for scarf base.

From green card stock, cut one 3/4-inch x 3-inch rectangle for hat band. Use compass to draw a 3/4-inch-diameter circle on white card stock and cut out for pompom on hat.

Use black marker to make decorative lines around edges of all cutout hat and scarf pieces. Run each piece through paper crimper. Set aside.

Cut a 2-inch square from black card stock and a 1-1/4-inch square from white card stock. Glue white piece centered on black piece for penguin's face.

Glue hat top piece to the top of face and glue scarf base to bottom of face. Glue scarf ends overlapping at an angle on right side of scarf.

Glue hat band to base of hat and glue pompom centered on top of hat. Glue wiggle eyes on upper face.

From orange card stock, cut a small triangle for the beak. Glue onto face centered below eyes.

Using cotton swab and blush, add a cheek on each side of beak. Using black marker, draw an eyebrow above each eye.

Glue penguin onto center of card front at a slight angle.

From white card stock, punch out five snowflakes. Glue one to each corner of card front. Glue remaining snowflake to the left side of scarf ends.

Either use a black marker or a computer and printer to print "HAVE A COOL YULE!" and "LET IT SNOW!" separately on green card stock. Cut a rectangle around each sentence, creating approximately 2-1/2-inch x 3/4-inch and 1-1/2-inch x 3/4-inch rectangles.

Use black marker to make decorative lines around edges of each printed green piece. Glue each onto card front.

Let card dry completely before placing in envelope. ❁

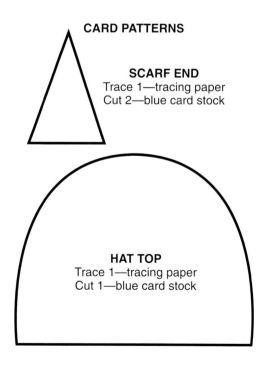

CARD PATTERNS

SCARF END
Trace 1—tracing paper
Cut 2—blue card stock

HAT TOP
Trace 1—tracing paper
Cut 1—blue card stock

Crocheted Mittens Bundle Up Trees

HANDS DOWN, Donna Collinsworth came up with a great idea for scrap yarn. From Lewis Center, Ohio, her ornaments are ideal for small gifts or for trimming a "giving tree" for charity.

MATERIALS NEEDED (for one):
Worsted-weight yarn—1 ounce each of two colors of your choice
Size H/8 (5mm) crochet hook
Yarn or tapestry needle
Scissors

FINISHED SIZE: Excluding hanging loop, each mitten is about 3 inches square.

DIRECTIONS:
CENTER STRIPE MITTEN: Round 1: With yarn A, ch 7, hdc 3rd ch from hk, hdc next 3 chs, 3 hdcs in last ch, turn, (now working across bottom of foundation ch) hdc next 3 sts, 2 hdcs in last st, sl st top beginning hdc, ch 1, turn (12 sts).

Rounds 2-3: Hdc in each st around, sl st top beginning hdc, ch 1, turn. End Round 3 and join yarn B, fasten off yarn A.

Rounds 4-5: Hdc in each st around, sl st top beginning hdc, ch 1, turn. End Round 5 and join yarn A, fasten off yarn B.

Rounds 6-7: Hdc in each st around, sl st top beginning hdc, ch 1, turn. End Round 7 and fasten off yarn.

THUMB FOR CENTER STRIPE MITTEN: With yarn A, ch 3, join with sl st in first ch to form a ring.

Round 1: Ch 1, work 6 hdcs into ring, sl st top beginning hdc, ch 1, turn (6 sts).

Rounds 2-4: Hdc in each st around, sl st top beginning hdc, ch 1, turn. End Round 4 and fasten off yarn.

With yarn A and needle, sew thumb to side of mitten.

HANGING LOOP: Row 1: With yarn A, ch 2, sc 2nd ch from hk, ch 1, turn (1 st).

Rows 2-8: Sc the only st, ch 1, turn. End Row 8 and fasten off yarn.

Fold hanger strip in half to form a loop. With yarn A and needle, sew to mitten underneath thumb.

ALTERNATING STRIPE MITTEN: Round 1: With yarn A, ch 7, hdc 3rd ch from hk, hdc next 3 chs, 3 hdcs in last ch, turn, (now working across bottom of foundation ch) hdc next 3 sts, 2 hdcs in last st, join yarn B, drop yarn A (do not fasten off), sl st top beginning hdc, ch 1, turn (12 sts).

Round 2: Hdc in each st around, pick up yarn A, drop yarn B, sl st top beginning hdc, ch 1, turn.

Round 3: Hdc in each st around, pick up yarn B, drop yarn A, sl st top beginning hdc, ch 1, turn.

Round 4: Hdc in each st around, pick up yarn A, drop yarn B, sl st top beginning hdc, ch 1, turn.

Round 5: Hdc in each st around, pick up yarn B, drop yarn A, sl st top beginning hdc, ch 1, turn.

Round 6: Hdc in each st around, pick up yarn A, fasten off yarn B, sl st top beginning hdc, ch 1, turn.

Round 7: Hdc in each st around, sl st top beginning hdc, fasten off yarn A.

THUMB FOR ALTERNATING STRIPE MITTEN: With yarn A, ch 3, join with sl st in first ch to form a ring.

Round 1: Ch 1, work 6 hdcs into ring, join yarn B, drop yarn A (do not fasten off), sl st top beginning hdc, ch 1, turn (6 sts).

Round 2: Hdc in each st around, pick up yarn A, drop yarn B, sl st top beginning hdc, ch 1, turn.

Round 3: Hdc in each st around, pick up yarn B, fasten off yarn A, sl st top beginning hdc, ch 1, turn.

Round 4: Hdc in each st around, sl st top beginning hdc, fasten off yarn B.

With yarn B and needle, sew thumb to side of mitten.

Following Hanging Loop directions, add hanging loop. ❄

ABBREVIATIONS			
ch(s)	chain(s)	hk	hook
sc(s)	single crochet(s)	sl st	slip stitch
hdc(s)	half double crochet(s)	st(s)	stitch(es)

10-inch length of 3/8-inch brown ribbon
Acrylic craft paints—dark red, flesh, blush, antique white,
    light brown, golden brown and black
Paper towels
Palette or foam plate
Water basin
Paintbrushes—small flat, 1/4-inch angle and liner
Fine sandpaper
Toothpicks
Glue gun and glue sticks
Clear tape
Standard sewing supplies

FINISHED SIZE: Santa decoration is approximately 8 inches
high by 5 inches wide.

DIRECTIONS:
Refer to the photo at left as a guide while creating the Santa
decoration as directed in the instructions that follow.

Trace pattern onto folded tracing paper with pencil.
Cut out along outline and unfold for complete pattern. From muslin, cut two Santa pieces.

With wrong sides together, edges matching and
beige thread, sew pieces together with a 1/4-inch
seam, leaving bottom open where shown on pattern. Turn right side out. Stuff firmly with polyester stuffing. Hand-sew opening closed.

PAINTING: Keep paper towels and a container of water handy to clean paintbrushes.
Place dabs of each color of paint onto palette
or foam plate as needed. Add coats of paint
as needed for complete coverage, letting
paint dry after each application.

Use flat brush and dark red to paint
Santa.

Use flat brush and flesh to paint center face area on one side of Santa about
2 inches below top point.

Use flat brush and antique white to
paint beard and mustache.

Use angle brush and blush to add
cheeks, lower lip, nose outline and
shading around edge of face.

Use angle brush and light
brown to outline edges of beard
and mustache. In same way, add
short strokes to inner beard.

Use flat brush and antique
white to paint hat trim around
Santa at top of head.

Use angle brush and
golden brown to paint small
mottled areas on hat trim for
dimension.

Dip end of paintbrush
handle into black and add
two small dots for eyes. In
same way, add five dots for buttons below beard.

Brush Up Decor
With Painted Santa

THE COLORS of Christmas really come through in this folksy
accent. "I sewed and painted a Santa, then surrounded him with a
wreath and trims," says Irene Wegener, of Corning, New York.

MATERIALS NEEDED:
Pattern on this page
Tracing paper and pencil
8-inch square of muslin
Polyester stuffing
All-purpose thread—beige and dark red
4-inch pine wreath
Pip berry sprigs with dark red and golden yellow berries
Five anise stars
Shredded wood excelsior
2-inch rusty metal star on wire
1/2-inch rusty jingle bell
3-inch-high mini wooden candy cane
Small matchbox
Dark green tissue paper

Grain

Foldline

SANTA PATTERN
Trace 1—
folded tracing paper
Cut 2—muslin

Leave
open

Use liner and antique white to paint eyebrows.

Dip toothpick into antique white and add highlight dots to eyes and wispy edges to hat trim. Dip another toothpick into light brown and add two dots to each button for holes.

Use flat brush and antique white to basecoat wooden candy cane. When dry, use angle brush and dark red to paint stripes about 1/4 inch apart on candy cane.

When dry, use sandpaper to remove paint randomly along edges of candy cane for a weathered look.

FINISHING: Using hand-sewing needle and dark red thread, sew bell to tip of hat.

Glue excelsior to center of wreath. Glue base of Santa to center of excelsior.

Glue pip berries on each side of Santa. Glue metal star among pip berries on left side of Santa.

Glue candy cane to lower left in front of Santa. Glue anise stars around candy cane bottom.

Wrap matchbox with green tissue paper and secure with clear tape on back. Tie brown ribbon around box so ribbon crisscrosses on front. Glue gift at an angle to lower right in front of Santa.

Let decoration dry completely. ❄

Christmas Tree Card Branches Out

AT THE ROOT of this design from Loretta Mateik, of Petaluma, California, is a die-cut shaped like an evergreen tree. "I set it off with a background of embossed holiday words," she says.

MATERIALS NEEDED:
Card stock—8-1/2-inch x 11-inch sheet of white and
   scraps each of red and gold
Rubber stamp of desired holiday words (Loretta used
   Hero Arts Merry Christmas/Happy New Year
   background stamp)
1/2-inch star punch
1-inch decorative corner punch
3-1/8-inch-high card stock die-cut shape—green pine tree
Clear embossing ink
Gold embossing powder
Embossing heat gun
Thin gold wire
Wire cutters
Scrapbook adhesive
Dimensional adhesive
Ruler
Scissors or paper trimmer
Envelope

FINISHED SIZE: Christmas card is 5-1/2 inches high x 4-1/4 inches wide.

DIRECTIONS:
Refer to the photo at right as a guide while assembling card as directed in the instructions that follow.

Cut white card stock in half widthwise and fold one piece to make a 5-1/2-inch x 4-1/4-inch side-folding card.

Using rubber stamp and clear embossing ink, stamp image onto the unfolded piece of white card stock. Sprinkle on gold embossing powder. Following heat gun manufacturer's instructions, emboss stamped area with heat gun. Trim card stock to a 3-1/2-inch x 4-1/2-inch rectangle.

From red card stock, cut a 3-7/8-inch x 5-inch rectangle. Use corner punch to punch each corner. Insert stamped piece into punched corners of red piece. Using scrapbook adhesive, attach the back of red piece to center front of folded card.

From gold card stock, punch two stars using star punch.

Using wire cutters, cut a 2-1/2-inch piece of gold wire. Use scrapbook adhesive to glue one end of wire between the two gold stars.

Curl remaining end of wire. Glue wire end to back of tree-top to suspend the star above tree.

Using dimensional adhesive, adhere the back of tree to center of stamped piece on front of card.

Let card dry completely before placing in envelope. ❄

Plastic shopping bags
Two bath towels
Palmolive dishwashing liquid without grease cutters
Magnetic purse closure amd two 2-inch squares of brown felt (optional)

FINISHED SIZE: Excluding handle, bag is about 12 inches high x 16 inches wide. Finished size may vary depending on felting.

DIRECTIONS:

KNITTING: The bag is made using double strands of yarn throughout. To double the strand, use outer yarn end on skein and pull the other yarn end from middle of skein.

Bottom: With Brown, cast on 44 sts.

Rows 1-20: K each row (44 sts).

Bind off.

Body: Round 1: With Brown, pick up 44 sts on long edge, place marker. Pick up 16 sts on short edge, place marker. Pick up 44 sts on other long edge, place marker. Pick up 16 stitches on other short edge, place 2 markers to denote the end of round (120 sts).

Rounds 2-4: K around (120 sts).

Rounds 5-41: With Emerald Green, k around (120 sts).

Round 42: With Ivory, k around (120 sts).

Rounds 43-45: With Brown, k around (120 sts).

Round 46: With Ivory, k around (120 sts).

Rounds 47-56: With Birds of Paradise, k around (120 sts).

Round 57: With Ivory, k around (120 sts).

Rounds 58-60: With Brown, k around (120 sts).

Round 61: With Ivory, k around (120 sts).

Rounds 62-67: With Emerald Green, work garter stitch (k 1 round, then p 1 round).

Bind off. Use needle to weave in loose ends.

I-cord strap (make two): With Emerald Green, cast on 5 sts. K across, do not turn. Slide sts to opposite end of needle, k across. Repeat until cord measures 30 to 36 inches according to desired length. With Emerald Green, sew the I-cord handle ends to top inner sides of bag before felting. Weave in loose ends.

FELTING: Place knit bag in pillowcase or laundry bag and close securely. Put in washing machine. Set machine to hot temperature and small size load. Add a bath towel and 1/4 cup of dishwashing liquid. Wash for 15 minutes. Remove from pillowcase and rinse with cold water. Gently squeeze out excess water. Do not put in dryer.

DRYING: Place bag on a dry towel on a protected surface. Shape bag and fill with crumpled plastic bags to maintain shape while drying. Remove plastic bags after 1-1/2 days. Let bag air-dry until completely dry.

FINISHING (OPTIONAL): Attach each side of the magnetic purse closure to the center of a 2-inch brown felt square. With brown yarn, hand-stitch the brown felt pieces opposite each other centered along the inside top edges of purse. ❈

Noel Gift Giving Is in the Bag

GET CARRIED AWAY with this felted knit tote—loved ones will be happy you did! "I'm making enough for my four daughters and daughter-in-law," says Mary Baker, of Glen Cove, New York.

MATERIALS NEEDED:

Paton's Classic Wool Yarn (100% wool)—2 skeins of Emerald Green and 1 skein each of Brown, Ivory and Birds of Paradise
24-inch-long size 13 circular knitting needles
Five stitch markers
Yarn or tapestry needle
Scissors
Pillowcase or laundry bag
Washing machine

ABBREVIATIONS	
st(s)	stitch(es)
k	knit
p	purl

Snowflake Frame Fits the Season

FALLING FLAKES can beautify the indoors, too—as this design proves! In Apollo, Pennsylvania, Sandy Rollinger decorated the see-through acrylic frame with white clay, beads and more for a frosty accent you'll want to keep out all winter long.

MATERIALS NEEDED:

8-inch x 10-inch clear plastic frame
4-inch x 6-inch rectangle of scrap card stock
8-inch x 10-inch rectangle of white card stock
Frosted glass finish
Pearl pigment powder (Sandy used Jacquard Pearl-Ex in Pearl White)
White oven-bake clay (Sandy used Sculpey Premo! Clay)
Swirl texture sheet or stamp
Plastic mat
Clay roller
Baking tray
Aluminum foil
Toaster oven or standard oven
2-1/4-inch snowflake cookie cutter
Decorative snow
Pallet knife
Small clear beads or pearls
Nine 3/4-inch white plastic snowflake shank buttons
Wire cutters
Small soft round paintbrush
Ruler
Scissors
Toothpicks
Tacky craft glue
Painter's tape
Clear tape
Desired 4-inch x 6-inch photo

FINISHED SIZE: Decorated frame is 8 inches wide x 10 inches high.

DIRECTIONS:

Refer to the photo at right as a guide while assembling frame as directed in the instructions that follow.

Condition white clay. Use clay roller to roll out clay to a 1/4-inch thickness on plastic mat.

Press the swirl sheet or stamp onto clay, leaving an impression. Use snowflake cookie cutter to cut three snowflakes from clay.

Place snowflakes on foil-lined baking tray. Using paintbrush, apply pigment powder to top of each snowflake. Bake according to clay manufacturer's instructions. Let cool.

Use painter's tape to adhere scrap card stock vertically to center front of frame. Following finish manufacturer's instructions, spray uncovered area on front of frame with frosted glass finish.

When dry, apply a second coat of frosted glass finish if desired. Let dry and remove card stock.

Use pallet knife to apply decorative snow around outer edges on front of frame. Repeat around unsprayed area in center of frame. Let dry.

Glue the clay snowflakes to sprayed area on front of frame. Let dry.

Using wire cutters, clip off shank on back of each snowflake button. Using toothpicks, apply a generous amount of glue to back of each button. Glue one button onto the center of each clay snowflake.

Glue remaining snowflake buttons randomly onto sprayed area on front of frame. Let dry.

Apply small dots of glue randomly onto sprayed area on front of frame. Place a clear bead or pearl on each dot of glue. Let dry.

Using clear tape, tape photo centered onto 8-inch x 10-inch piece of white card stock. Place in frame so photo shows through unsprayed area in center of frame. ❀

CROSS-STITCHING: Zigzag or overcast the edges of the Aida cloth to prevent fraying. To find the center of the Aida cloth, fold it in half crosswise, then fold it in half lengthwise and mark where the folds intersect.

Draw lines across the chart, connecting opposite arrows. Mark where lines intersect. Begin stitching here for a centered design.

Each square on the chart represents one set of fabric threads surrounded by four holes. Each stitch is worked over one set of threads with the tapestry needle passing through the holes.

The color and/or symbol inside each square on the chart, along with the color key, indicates which color of six-strand embroidery floss to use to make cross-stitches. Wide lines on the chart show where to make backstitches. For the tree star, make a Smyrna cross. For the bear eyes, make French knots. See Fig. 1 at top right for stitch illustrations.

Use 18-inch lengths of floss. Longer strands tend to tangle and fray. Separate the strands of floss and thread the needle with two strands for all cross-stitches. Use one strand for backstitches, the Smyrna cross and French knots.

To begin stitching, leave a 1-inch tail of floss on back of work and hold tail in place while working the first few stitches over it. To end stitching, run the needle under a few stitches in back before clipping the floss close to work.

FINISHING: Trace pattern onto folded tracing paper with pencil. Cut out along outline and open for complete pattern. Cut one house each from cardboard, fleece and felt.

Glue fleece on top of cardboard with edges matching. Let dry. Center stitched design right side up on fleece. Wrap edges of stitched piece around to back of cardboard and glue, making sure to smooth the fabric. Let dry.

For the hanging loop, form ribbon piece into a loop and glue the loose ends to the top back of cardboard. Let dry.

Glue the felt centered on back of ornament. Let dry. ❀

Homey Stitching Welcomes St. Nick

CELEBRATE SANTA coming down the chimney with this cute cross-stitching. Created by Renee Dent, of Conrad, Montana, the house-shaped accent makes a festive trim anywhere.

MATERIALS NEEDED:
Chart and pattern on next page
Tracing paper and pencil
6-inch x 7-inch piece of ecru 18-count Aida cloth
DMC six-strand embroidery floss in colors listed on color key
Size 24 tapestry needle
5-inch x 6-inch piece each of lightweight cardboard, Pellon fleece and green felt
6-inch length of 1/8-inch green satin ribbon
Tacky craft glue
Scissors

FINISHED SIZE: Excluding hanging loop, ornament measures about 4-3/4 inches high x 4-3/8 inches wide. Design area is 57 stitches high x 66 stitches wide.

DIRECTIONS:
Refer to the photo above as a guide while creating the ornament as directed in the instructions that follow.

COLOR KEY	DMC
⦿ White	
◎ Ecru	
◣ Very Dark Shell Pink	221
◼ Black	310
✪ Very Dark Baby Blue	312
◨ Red	321
◧ Light Brown	434
◘ Dark Red	498
◉ Very Light Pearl Gray	762
⊞ Medium Pink	776
☐ Medium Topaz	783
☒ Very Light Beige Brown	842
✿ Very Dark Parrot Green	904
▣ Light Tawny	951
◖ Dark Golden Brown	975
◼ Dark Hunter Green	3345
◪ Very Dark Old Gold	3829
BACKSTITCH	
☐ White (glint in eyes)	
▬ Black	310
▬ Very Light Beige Brown	842
SMYRNA CROSS	
▬ Dark Lemon (tree star)	444
FRENCH KNOT	
▬ Black (bear eyes)	310

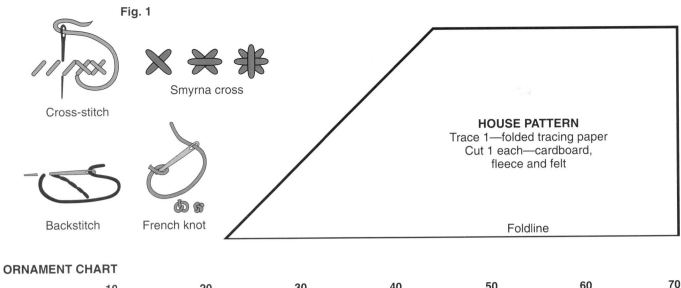

Fig. 1

Cross-stitch

Smyrna cross

Backstitch

French knot

HOUSE PATTERN
Trace 1—folded tracing paper
Cut 1 each—cardboard,
fleece and felt

Foldline

ORNAMENT CHART

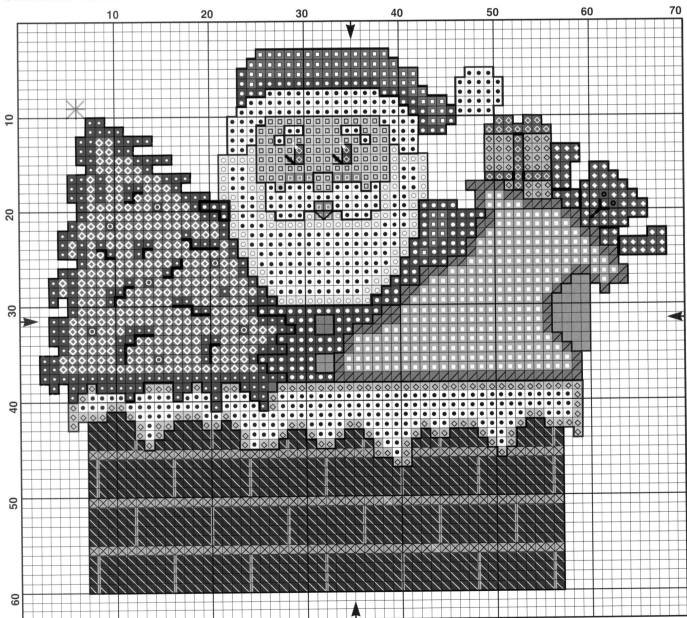

Craft knife
Cutting board or self-healing cutting mat
Small stencil brush
Small paintbrush
Paper towels
Palette or foam plate
Water basin
Acrylic craft paints (Lenora used Deco Art Americana)—
    Blueberry and Cadmium Yellow
Permanent fabric glue (Lenora used Fabri-Tac)
Spray adhesive
Dark blue six-strand embroidery floss
Embroidery needle
Embroidery hoop
Rectangle of cardboard to fit 8-inch x 10-inch opening of
    photo frame
Clear tape
Scissors
Iron and ironing board

FINISHED SIZE: Wall decoration is approximately 8 inches wide by 10 inches high.

DIRECTIONS:
Refer to the photo at left as a guide while creating wall decoration as directed in the instructions that follow.

Use pencil to trace stencil pattern onto stencil blank or card stock. Using craft knife and cutting board or mat, cut out pattern design to form stencil.

EMBROIDERY: Use a pencil to lightly trace "Noel" pattern onto the muslin, positioning the top of pattern about 1-3/4 inches below top 8-inch edge of muslin and centering the pattern horizontally.

Place muslin in embroidery hoop with the "Noel" pattern centered. Separate dark blue six-strand floss and thread embroidery needle with three strands. Stitch "Noel" using a running stitch. See Fig. 1 at top far right for stitch illustration.

Remove muslin from embroidery hoop and press.

PAINTING: Keep paper towels and a container of water handy to clean the paintbrushes. Place dabs of each color of paint onto palette or foam plate as needed.

Place manger stencil on top of muslin, positioning bottom of pattern about 1-3/4 inches above bottom 8-inch edge of muslin and centering the pattern horizontally. Lightly tape outer edges of stencil to muslin to secure.

Using Blueberry paint and stencil brush, paint manger design onto muslin. Remove stencil. Let dry.

Using Cadmium Yellow and small paintbrush, add straw by painting short strokes freehand below Baby Jesus along the top edge of manger.

Using Cadmium Yellow and small paintbrush, paint three small stars freehand at random in the space above Baby Jesus. Let dry.

FINISHING: Tear fabric scraps into strips of various sizes. Arrange strips along front edges of muslin and between the embroidered and stenciled designs as desired. Using fabric glue, adhere fabric strips to muslin. Let dry.

With edges matching, attach cardboard piece to back of muslin using spray adhesive. Let dry. Place into frame. ❈

Framed Accent Has Christmas Spirit

HOW DIVINE—Pella, Iowa crafter Lenora Schut made a stencil of Baby Jesus in the manger and used it to embellish plain muslin. Embroidery and homey fabrics complete her folksy design.

MATERIALS NEEDED:
Patterns on next page
Pencil
Desired photo frame with 8-inch x 10-inch opening
Rectangle of unbleached muslin to fit 8-inch x 10-inch
    opening of photo frame
Desired fabric scraps
4-inch-square stencil blank or piece of card stock

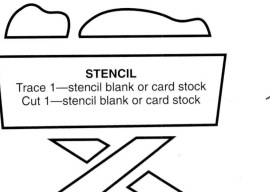

STENCIL
Trace 1—stencil blank or card stock
Cut 1—stencil blank or card stock

Fig. 1
Running stitch

EMBROIDERY
Trace 1—muslin
Stitch as directed in instructions

Snowy Seeds Will Plant Winter Cheer

HAVE GARDENERS or snowman lovers on your Christmas list? Give them a gift that's sure to grow smiles—this cute basket filled with frosty "seeds" from Irene Wegener, of Corning, New York.

MATERIALS NEEDED:
Small basket with handle (basket shown measures about
   3-1/2 inches tall by 3 inches in diameter)
Three 3/4-inch wooden balls
Small wooden tag
Small decorative snow shovel
1-inch x 6-inch strip of plaid fabric
Three clear plastic or white wooden 1-1/2-inch
   snowflakes
Acrylic craft paints—white, black, dark orange, blush, tan
   and dark brown
Paper towels
Palette or foam plate
Water basin
Paintbrushes—small flat and small dry
Snow-Tex glittering snow
Green-colored wood excelsior
Toothpicks
Glue gun and glue sticks
Ultrafine black permanent marker

FINISHED SIZE: Decorated basket shown is approximately 4 inches tall by 4-1/2 inches wide.

DIRECTIONS:
Refer to the photo at right as a guide while creating the basket as directed in the instructions that follow.

PAINTING: Keep paper towels and a container of water handy to clean paintbrushes. Place dabs of each color of paint onto palette or foam plate as needed. Add coats of paint as needed for complete coverage, letting paint dry after each application.

Use flat brush and white to paint wooden balls.

Apply a thin coat of glittering snow all over white balls. Let dry.

Using toothpick and black, add two dots for eyes and five smaller dots for mouth on each ball.

Use toothpick and dark orange to add a dot for the nose on each ball. When dry, use dry brush and blush to add the cheeks.

Use flat brush and tan to paint wooden tag. When dry, use flat brush and dark brown to lightly shade outer edges on front of tag.

Use permanent marker to write "Snowman Seeds Plant With Love" on center front of tag. In same way, add dashed line around edge on front of tag. Let dry.

FINISHING: Glue a handful of excelsior in basket bottom. Glue snowflakes in back of basket and glue snowman balls in front of basket with faces upward. Let dry.

Thread fabric strip through tag hole. Loosely tie tag around basket handle. Insert shovel into fabric tie. Tighten and knot fabric strip to secure tag and shovel. ❄

Place Mat Makes A Tasteful Table

SERVE UP this Christmasy covering, and you're sure to delight holiday guests. "I added a holly applique to one corner of a simple pieced design," says Loretta Mateik, of Petaluma, California.

MATERIALS NEEDED (for one):
Patterns on next page
Tracing paper
Pencil
Paper-backed fusible web
44-inch-wide 100% cotton fabric—1/8 yard of dark red print for inner border blocks; 1/8 yard of light red print for inner border blocks; 1/4 yard of speckled green print for center block and holly leaves; 1/8 yard of green leaf print for outer border corner blocks; 1/2 yard of dark red solid for inner border blocks, backing and upper holly berries; 1/4 yard of medium red solid for inner border blocks, outer border strips and lower holly berry; and 1/4 yard of medium green solid for inner border strips
All-purpose thread to match fabrics
Six-strand embroidery floss—dark red, medium red, light green and medium green
Embroidery needle
Quilter's marking pen or pencil
Quilter's ruler
Rotary cutter and mat
Standard sewing supplies

FINISHED SIZE: Place mat is approximately 18-1/2 inches wide x 14 inches high.

DIRECTIONS:
Prewash fabrics, washing each color separately. If rinse water is discolored, wash again until rinse water runs clear. Dry and press fabrics.

CUTTING: Use rotary cutter and quilter's ruler to cut fabrics as follows:

From speckled green print, cut one 5-1/2-inch x 8-inch rectangle for center block.

From dark red print, cut three 2-1/2-inch x 3-inch rectangles for inner border blocks.

From light red print, cut two 2-1/2-inch x 3-inch rectangles and two 3-inch squares for inner border blocks.

From dark red solid, cut three 2-1/2-inch x 3-inch rectangles and one 3-inch square for inner border blocks. Also cut one 14-1/2-inch x 19-inch rectangle for the backing.

From medium red solid, cut two 2-1/2-inch x 3-inch rectangles and one 3-inch square for inner border blocks. Also cut two 2-1/2-inch x 11-1/2-inch strips and two 2-inch x 15-inch strips for outer border.

From medium green solid, cut two 1-1/2-inch x 9-1/2-inch strips and two 1-1/2-inch x 15-inch strips for green inner border.

From green leaf print, cut four 2-1/2-inch x 2-inch rectangles for outer border corners.

PIECING: Refer to photo above and placement diagram at right for placement. Do all stitching with right sides of fabric together, edges even, matching thread and an accurate 1/4-inch seam. Press seams toward darker fabrics.

Row 1: Sew five 2-1/2-inch x 3-inch rectangles together along short edges in the following order—dark red solid, dark red print, medium red solid, light red print and dark red solid.

Row 2: Sew together a 3-inch light red print square and a 3-inch dark red solid square along one edge. Make a second strip in same way using a 3-inch light red print square and a 3-inch medium red solid square. Sew the first set of squares to the left short side of the 5-1/2-inch x 8-inch speckled green print rectangle. Sew the second set to the right short side of same rectangle.

Row 3: Sew five 2-1/2-inch x 3-inch rectangles together along short edges in the following order—light red print, medium red solid, dark red print, dark red solid and dark red print.

Center block: Sew Row 1 to the top of Row 2. Sew Row 3 to the bottom of Row 2.

Green inner border: Sew the short medium green solid strips to opposite short sides of center block. Sew the long medium green solid strips to top and bottom of center block.

Outer border: Sew the short medium red solid strips to opposite short sides of medium green inner border. Sew a 2-1/2-inch x 2-inch green leaf rectangle to each short end of each remaining medium red solid strip, then sew pieced strips to top and bottom of place mat.

APPLIQUES: Trace patterns separately onto tracing paper with pencil.

Trace three berries and three leaves onto paper side of fusible web, leaving at least 1/2 inch between the shapes. Cut shapes apart, leaving a margin of paper around each.

Following web manufacturer's instructions, fuse leaves onto wrong side of the speckled green print. In same way, fuse two berries onto dark red solid and fuse remaining berry onto medium red solid.

When cool, cut out the shapes along the pattern outlines. Remove paper backing. Referring to photo for position, fuse leaves and berries to place mat.

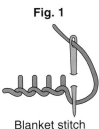

Fig. 1

Blanket stitch

EMBROIDERY: Separate six-strand floss and thread needle with the number of strands indicated in the instructions that follow. See Fig. 1 at right for stitch illustration.

Using two strands of medium red floss, blanket stitch around the medium red berry.

Using two strands of dark red floss, blanket stitch around the two dark red berries.

Using two strands of medium green floss and one strand of light green floss, blanket stitch around the center leaf.

Using two strands of medium green floss, blanket stitch around the two outer leaves.

FINISHING: Pin the 14-1/2-inch x 19-inch dark red backing piece centered to the finished top piece with right sides together. Sew around the edges using a 1/4-inch seam, leaving approximately 7 inches open for turning. Clip seams and turn. Hand sew opening closed. ✿

PLACE MAT PATTERNS
Trace 1 each—tracing paper

HOLLY LEAF
Cut 3—fused speckled green print

HOLLY BERRY
Cut 2—fused dark red solid
Cut 1—fused medium red solid

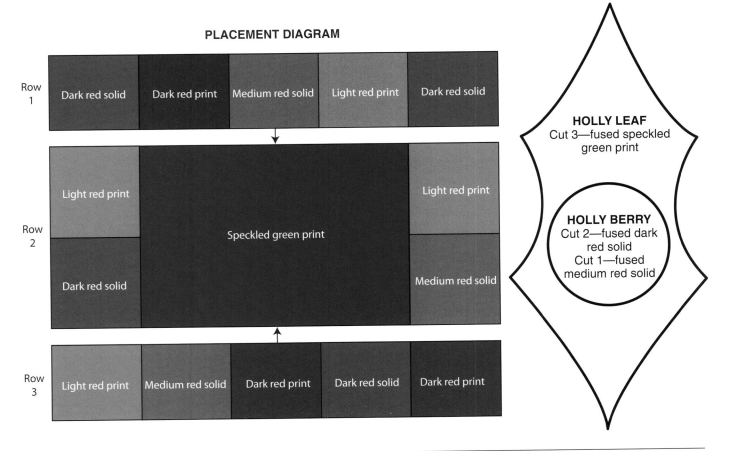

PLACEMENT DIAGRAM

| Row 1 | Dark red solid | Dark red print | Medium red solid | Light red print | Dark red solid |

Row 2: Light red print, Speckled green print, Light red print, Dark red solid, Medium red solid

Row 3: Light red print, Medium red solid, Dark red print, Dark red solid, Dark red print

Melt Hearts With Frosty Ornaments

BUILDING snowmen in a craft room can be just as fun as going outdoors. "I used colorful clay to shape these cute characters for the tree," says Apollo, Pennsylvania's Sandy Rollinger.

MATERIALS NEEDED (for both):
Pattern on this page
Tracing paper and pencil
Oven-bake clay (Sandy used Sculpey III)—Blue, Granny Smith, Pearl, Spring Lilac, Black, Just Orange and Dusty Rose
3-1/2-inch canning lid ring or circle cookie cutter not used for food
Plastic mat
Craft knife
Clay blade
Clay roller
Aluminum foil
Baking tray
Toaster oven or standard oven
Unused scrubby pad
Decorative snow
White dimensional paint
Ruler
Toothpick
Two 8-inch lengths of white string

FINISHED SIZE: Excluding hanging loop, each ornament is approximately 3-1/2 inches in diameter.

DIRECTIONS:
Refer to the photo at left as a guide while assembling ornaments as directed in the instructions that follow.

Condition all clay. Use clay roller to roll out all clay to a 1/4-inch thickness on plastic mat.

ORNAMENT BASES: Use canning lid ring or cookie cutter to cut two circles from Blue clay. Add texture to front of circles with scrubby pad.

Using toothpick, create a small hole near the edge of each clay circle for a hanging loop to be added later.

Trace the snowman pattern onto tracing paper with pencil and cut out. Place pattern on a sheet of Pearl clay and use craft knife to cut around pattern. Flip pattern over and cut around pattern again to create another snowman facing the opposite direction.

Place each snowman onto a circle base so that the bottom of each snowman is about 1/2 inch from bottom of circle and the hole in base is at the top. Gently press into place.

STRIPED SNOWMAN: Scarf/hat: For scarf base, use clay blade to cut two 1/2-inch-high triangles and two slightly curving 1-inch-high triangles from Spring Lilac clay.

Use clay blade to cut thin strips from Granny Smith clay. Gently press on top of scarf base pieces to form stripes. Place striped scarf pieces onto neck area of right-facing snowman. Gently shape and press into place.

Roll pea-size ball of Granny Smith clay. Place where scarf triangles meet and gently press to flatten.

For hat base, use clay blade to cut a 1/4-inch x 3/4-inch rectangle from Spring Lilac clay and pinch one end smaller. In same way, cut a 1-inch-long smile shape for hat brim.

Use clay blade to cut a thin strip from Granny Smith clay for hatband. Place the hat pieces on head and gently press into place.

Face/body: Using Just Orange clay, roll a 1/2-inch-long narrow cone shape for the carrot nose. Using Dusty Rose clay, roll a very small ball for cheek.

Using Black clay, roll a very thin 1/4-inch-long string for mouth, two very small balls for eyes, two pea-size balls for buttons and several tiny strings to form arm branches.

Place all face/body pieces on snowman and gently press into place.

POLKA-DOT SNOWMAN: Scarf/hat: Roll small balls of Dusty Rose clay and press onto sheet of Granny Smith clay to form a polka-dot pattern. Use roller to embed balls into clay.

For scarf base, use clay blade to cut two 1/2-inch-high triangles and two 1-inch-high triangles from polka-dot Granny Smith clay. Place scarf pieces onto neck area of left-facing snowman. Gently shape and press into place.

Roll pea-size ball of Granny Smith clay. Place where scarf

SNOWMAN PATTERN
Trace 1—
tracing paper
Cut as directed
in instructions

triangles meet and gently press to flatten.

For hat base, use clay blade to cut a 1-1/2-inch-high triangle from polka-dot Granny Smith clay. Place onto head, shaping hat into a curve. Gently press into place.

Roll pea-size ball of Pearl clay for pompom. Place at end of hat and gently flatten.

Face/body: Follow the face/body instructions for Striped Snowman.

FINISHING: Place snowmen ornaments on foil-lined bak-ing tray. Bake according to clay manufacturer's instructions. Let cool.

Insert one string through hole at top of each ornament. Tie each string into a loop for hanging.

Place ornaments onto sheet of foil. Apply decorative snow below snowmen and around edge on front of each circle base. Let dry.

For snowflakes, add dots of white dimensional paint to circle base and hats. Let dry. ❄

Silver Earrings Are Simply Sensational

HAVE YOU HEARD? It's a snap to assemble your own elegant earrings. Just try this pretty design featuring dangling chains from Sarah Farley, of Menomonee Falls, Wisconsin.

MATERIALS NEEDED:
Two silver French earring hooks
Two 4mm clear crystals
Two small silver cone caps
Two 36-inch lengths of silver chain
Two 3-inch lengths of fine silver wire
Wire cutters
Ruler
Round-nose pliers
Needle-nose pliers

FINISHED SIZE: Excluding the hook, each earring is about 2-3/4 inches long.

DIRECTIONS:
Refer to the photo at right as a guide while making the earrings as directed in the instructions that follow.

CUTTING: Using wire cutters, cut one 36-inch length of chain into the following lengths in order: 1-7/16 inches, 1-11/16 inches, 1-3/16 inches, 1-7/8 inches, 1/2 inch, 1-1/4 inches, 2 inches, 1-5/8 inches, 1-3/4 inches, 3/4 inch, 1-11/16 inches, 2-1/16 inches, 1-7/8 inches, 3/4 inch, 1-3/8 inches, 1-5/8 inches, 1-3/8 inches, 1-1/8 inches, 7/8 inch, 2 inches, 7/8 inch, 1-1/8 inches and 1-3/4 inches.

Repeat with the remaining 36-inch length of chain, keeping the two sets of cut chain pieces separate.

ASSEMBLY (for each earring): Bend one 3-inch length of fine wire about an inch from an end so it resembles a check mark. String one set of cut chain pieces in order onto the short end of the 3-inch wire.

Bend the wire piece at the crease, bringing the two ends together. Using the needle-nose pliers, wrap the short end 3-4 times around the long end of wire. Cut off the excess from the short end with wire cutters.

String one cone cap and then one 4mm clear crystal onto the remaining long end of wire.

Using needle-nose pliers, bend the wire end at a right angle, leaving a little space above the crystal. Place the round-nose pliers about 1/4 inch from the crease and bend the wire

to make a loop. While holding the loop with the round-nose pliers, use needle-nose pliers to wrap the excess wire around the stem 3-4 times, making the crystal and cone fit tightly. Cut off the excess with wire cutters.

Using needle-nose pliers, pull the loop on a French hook slightly open. Slip the loop of newly formed earring onto French hook loop. Using needle-nose pliers, close the French hook loop to secure the earring.

Repeat assembly to create another earring. ❄

Ornaments Feature Holiday Character

PUT A FESTIVE FACE on the Christmas season with these fun tree ornaments. In Petaluma, California, Loretta Mateik created a simple Santa Claus, Rudolph and jolly elf in a snap.

MATERIALS NEEDED:
(For all):
Tacky craft glue
Ruler
Cotton swabs
(For Santa):
Unfinished wood pieces—2-1/2-inch circle, two 1/2-inch
    circles, 3-1/4-inch x 1-3/4-inch oval, two 1-3/4-inch x
    3/4-inch candy canes and 5/8-inch mushroom button
Drill with 1/16-inch bit
Acrylic craft paints—flesh, white, black, terra-cotta, red
    and slate gray
Paintbrushes—medium flat and liner
Paper towels
Water basin
Palette or foam plate
6-1/2-inch length of black embroidery floss
(For reindeer):
Patterns on next page
Tracing paper and pencil
2-3/4-inch-wide x 2-3/8-inch-high clay pot
Unfinished wood pieces—3/4-inch circle and 3/8-inch
    mushroom button

Drill with 1/16-inch bit
Scraps of craft foam—dark brown and light brown
Acrylic craft paints—white, black, red and terra-cotta
Paintbrushes—medium flat and liner
Paper towels
Water basin
Palette or foam plate
3-1/2-inch length of small-gauge wire
3/4-inch jingle bell
1-1/2-inch length of black embroidery floss
Scissors
(For elf):
Patterns on next page
Tracing paper and pencil
Card stock—12-inch x 6-inch green rectangle and scrap
    of cream
1-inch x 8-inch strip of quilt batting
10-inch length of 1/8-inch red satin ribbon
Red chalk
Stapler
Black permanent fine-line marker
Dimensional foam adhesive
Scissors

FINISHED SIZE: Excluding hanging loops, Santa is 3-1/2 inches wide x 2-7/8 inches high, reindeer is 3 inches wide x 2-3/8 inches high and elf is 3 inches wide x 4-1/4 inches high.

DIRECTIONS:
Refer to the photo above as a guide while creating ornaments as directed in the instructions that follow.

Keep paper towels and a container of water handy to clean the paintbrushes. Place dabs of each color of paint onto palette or foam plate as needed. Add coats of paint as needed for complete coverage, letting paint dry after each application.

SANTA: Using 1/16-inch bit, drill a hole about 1/4 inch from the edge on the large wood circle.

Using flat brush and flesh, basecoat the large circle, 5/8-inch mushroom button and two small circles.

Using flat brush and white, basecoat the oval and candy canes.

Using flat brush and terra-cotta, lightly shade around the entire outer edge of the large circle and one half of the outer top edge of mushroom button.

Using flat brush and slate gray, shade the outer edges of the candy canes and one half of the outer edge of oval.

Dip the end of paintbrush handle into black. Add two small dots about 1/2 inch below drilled hole on large circle for eyes, pulling brush down slightly to elongate eyes into ovals.

Using liner and black, add the mouth, beard lines, eyebrows, lines of eyes and a curved line on each small circle.

Using liner and white, add a very small dot to bottom of each eye and a curved highlight at top of mushroom button.

Dip cotton swab into red and wipe off excess paint. Lightly dab two small circles on large circle for cheeks.

Use tacky craft glue to glue small circles on back outer edge of large circle for ears.

For mustache, glue candy canes on white oval so that the straight ends meet above mouth. Glue mushroom button on top of straight candy cane ends for nose. Glue oval to bottom half of large circle, about 1/4 inch below the eyes. Let dry.

Thread one end of floss through drilled hole. Tie ends together to form a loop for hanging.

REINDEER: Using 1/16-inch bit, drill a hole through center of 3/8-inch mushroom button from bottom to top.

Use flat brush and terra-cotta to basecoat mushroom button and clay pot.

Use flat brush and red to basecoat wood circle for nose.

Use liner and black to add the eyes and eyebrows centered on one side of pot.

Dip cotton swab into red and wipe off excess paint. Lightly dab two small circles on pot for cheeks.

Use liner and white to add a very small dot to bottom of each eye and a curved highlight to top of nose.

Trace antler and ear patterns onto tracing paper with pencil and cut out. Cut from craft foam as directed on patterns.

Fold edge of each ear over as shown on pattern and glue in place. Let dry. Glue antlers on opposite sides of face on pot. Glue ears in front of antlers. Let dry.

Apply glue to straight edges of mushroom button, then insert button into hole in bottom of pot from the inside so that the rounded end of button is inside pot.

Fold wire about 1 inch from one end and wrap the wire around itself to form a loop. Thread opposite end of wire through hole in mushroom button so that the loop is inside pot. Thread end of wire back down through hole in button, forming a large loop on top of pot for hanger. Twist end around top of small inner loop to secure outer loop in place.

Thread one end of floss through top of bell and thread opposite end through loop inside pot. Tie floss ends together so that the bell hangs slightly above edge of pot.

ELF: Mark center point along one long edge of green card stock rectangle. Draw lines from center point to each corner on opposite edge. Cut along lines, forming a large triangle.

Roll large triangle into a cone shape by rolling one short edge to the opposite short edge, leaving a small opening at top of cone to insert hanger later. Staple overlapping edges of cone to secure in place. Trim excess paper from wide end of cone to create an even circular rim.

Trace face and nose patterns separately onto tracing paper with pencil and cut out. Cut each from cream card stock.

Using marker, draw the eyes and eyebrows on face and the highlight on nose.

Using cotton swab and red chalk, apply cheeks to face.

Use tacky craft glue to glue face to front of cone, leaving ears unglued and aligning bottom edges of face and cone. Referring to pattern for position, fold ears slightly forward.

Use dimensional foam adhesive to attach nose centered below eyes.

Use tacky craft glue to adhere batting along top edge of face and around to back of cone for the hat brim, allowing the ears to slightly overlap brim. Trim ends of strip if necessary.

Knot ends of ribbon to form a loop. Insert untied end into opening at top of cone from the inside outward. Pull loop through until knot rests against inside top of cone. ❀

ORNAMENT PATTERNS
Trace 1 each—tracing paper

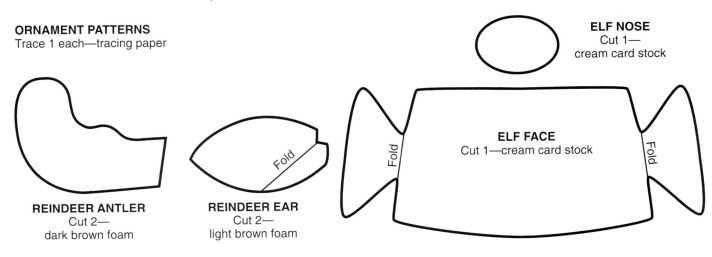

ELF NOSE
Cut 1—
cream card stock

ELF FACE
Cut 1—cream card stock

Fold

Fold

Fold

REINDEER ANTLER
Cut 2—
dark brown foam

REINDEER EAR
Cut 2—
light brown foam

Chase Away Chills With Cozy Sweater

WINTER WEATHER is no match for this pretty purple pullover. "I just love to knit," writes Sarah McFarland from Burdett, New York. "I added cables to this design as an embellishment."

MATERIALS NEEDED:

Worsted-weight yarn in desired color (Sarah used Bear Farm Yarns Worsted)—five (six for large-size sweater) 4-ounce skeins
Knitting needles—16-inch-long size 9 circular needle, 24-inch-long size 9 circular needle, one set of five size 9 double-pointed needles, 16-inch-long size 8 circular needle and one set of five size 8 double-pointed needles
Size H/8 (4.5 mm) crochet hook
Cable needle
Eight stitch markers
Two large stitch holders or long pieces of scrap yarn

GAUGE: Working in stockinette stitch, 16 sts and 23 rows = 4 inches. To save time, take time to check gauge.

TECHNIQUES/STITCHES USED:

Cable Twist (CT):
   Place 2 sts on cable needle and hold at back of work. K2, k2 from cable needle.
Ssk:
   Slip 1 knitwise, slip 1 knitwise, k the 2 slipped sts together through back loop (decrease).
Make 1 (m1):
   To increase one stitch, use the left needle to lift horizontal strand lying between the two needles, twist the strand and knit it.

FINISHED SIZE: Directions are for Women's size Small/Medium with changes for Women's size Large in parentheses. The Small/Medium size measures about 40 inches around the chest and 24 inches in length. The Large size measures about 45 inches around the chest and 27 inches in length.

DIRECTIONS:

Using 16-inch size 9 circular needle, cast on 100 (112) sts. Join, being careful not to twist. Begin working in the round.

   YOKE: Round 1: °K26 (30) sts, pm, p2, k4, p2, pm, k8 (10), pm, p2, k4, p2, pm, repeat from ° once. This begins a front, back and two sleeves with four cable sections to divide them. Use a different color marker at the beginning of the round to keep track.

   Round 2: K the k sts and p the p sts. Stop at the marker at the beginning of the round.

   Round 3 (Increase Round): °K2, m1, k until 2 sts before marker, m1, k2, sm, p2, k4, p2, sm, repeat from ° to end of round: 108 (120) sts.

   Round 4 (Cable Round): °K to marker, sm, p2, CT, p2, sm, repeat from ° to end of round.

   Round 5 (Increase Round): °K2, m1, k until 2 sts before marker, m1, k2, sm, p2, k4, p2, sm, repeat from ° to end of round.

   Rounds 6-49 (6-57): Switch to 24-inch size 9 circular needle when stitches become too crowded. Repeat Yoke Rounds 2-5 eleven (thirteen) more times: 292 (336) sts, divided as 82 (94) sts in the chest and back sections (counting from center of cable) and 64 (74) sts in each arm section.

   Rounds 50-56 (58-64): K the k sts and p the p sts, making no increases or CTs.

   SEPARATE BODY AND SLEEVES: K to first marker, p2, k2. Slip next 64 (74) sts onto large stitch holder or long piece of scrap yarn. Continue to work next 82 (94) stitches of front. Slip next 64 (74) sts onto large stitch holder or long piece of scrap yarn. K2, p2.

   BODY: Rounds 1-7: K the k sts and p the p sts: 164 (188) sts. This is to create ease under the arms without adding bulk.

   Round 8: °K to marker, sm, p2, CT, p2, sm, repeat from ° to end of round.

   Rounds 9-11: K the k sts and p the p sts.

   Rounds 12-75 (12-91): Repeat Body Rounds 8-11 sixteen (twenty) more times or to within 2 inches of desired length.

   WAIST RIBBING: Round 1: At beginning of round, switch to size 8 circular needle. °K2, p2 to marker, sm, p2, CT, p2, sm, repeat from ° to end of round.

   Rounds 2-4: °K2, p2, repeat from ° around.

   Rounds 5-12: Repeat Waist Ribbing Rounds 1-4 two times (ribbing is approximately 2 inches long; continue up to 4 inches if desired). Bind off all sts loosely.

SLEEVES: Place the 64 (74) sts from the stitch holder or scrap yarn onto the 16-inch size 9 circular needle.

Round 1: K2, k the next 2 p sts together, k56 (66), k the next 2 p sts together, k2, pm for beginning/end of sleeve round.

Rounds 2-6: K all sts.

Round 7: K1, k2tog, knit to 3 sts before marker, ssk, k1.

Rounds 8-49 (8-61): Repeat Sleeves Rounds 2-7 seven (nine) more times. Switch to size 9 double-pointed needles when the sleeve becomes too narrow to work on circular needles: 48 sts. K remaining stitches until within 2 inches of desired length.

SLEEVE RIBBING: Switch to size 8 double-pointed needles. Work in K2, p2 ribbing for 10 rounds. Bind off loosely.

NECK: With crochet hook and size 8 double-pointed needles, pick up 100 (112) sts around neckline. Work in k2, p2 ribbing for 10 rounds or, for a fold-over turtleneck, work in k2, p2 ribbing for about 10 inches.

Bind off all sts loosely. Weave in all loose ends. Block to measurements. ❄

Snowman Shows a Craving for Sweets

WHIP UP this merry mug to decorate your home all winter long. In Corning, New York, Irene Wegener displays a love of hot cocoa and cookies with this whimsical stitched snowman.

MATERIALS NEEDED:
Pattern on page 104
Tracing paper and pencil
Two 3-inch x 5-inch rectangles of white flannel
White all-purpose thread
Polyester stuffing
Two 3mm black beads for eyes
Six-strand embroidery floss—black and red
Embroidery needle
1-inch x 8-inch torn strip of plaid fabric
Paper towels
Water container
Foam plate or palette
Acrylic craft paints—black, black cherry, burnt orange, toffee brown, antique gold, red, antique white
Paintbrushes—small flat, old scruffy brush and liner
Two toothpicks
2-3/8-inch-high white enamel mug with black trim
1/4-inch-thick wood cutouts—one 1/2-inch-high star and one 1-5/8-inch-high gingerbread man
Cotton swab
Powdered cosmetic blush
Black fine-line marker
Spanish moss
Three 4-inch-long pieces of narrow wired pine garland
Miniature decorative shovel
Three red pip berry stems
Glue gun and glue sticks

FINISHED SIZE: Snowman mug measures about 6 inches high x 4-1/2 inches wide.

DIRECTIONS:
Refer to the photo at right while assembling snowman mug as directed in the instructions that follow.

SNOWMAN: Trace snowman pattern onto tracing paper with pencil as directed on pattern.

Pin the two pieces of white flannel together with right sides together and edges matching. Pin the snowman pattern to layered flannel.

With white thread and a short straight stitch, sew on pattern outline, leaving an opening for turning where shown on pattern. Remove pattern.

Trim excess fabric, leaving a narrow seam.

Turn snowman right side out and stuff firmly.

Turn in raw edges of opening and hand-sew closed.

Separate black six-strand floss and thread embroidery needle with two strands. Insert needle through back of snowman's neck to sew black beads to snowman for eyes. In same way, use running stitches to add mouth. See Fig. 1 on page 104 for stitch illustrations.

Use cotton swab and a circular motion to add cosmetic blush to snowman's cheeks.

Thread embroidery needle with unseparated red floss. Insert needle through back of snowman's neck and stitch two star shapes on front of snowman.

PAINTING: Keep paper towels and a container of water handy to clean paintbrushes. Place small amounts of paint as needed onto foam plate or palette. Add coats of paint as

(Continued on next page)

needed for complete coverage, letting the paint dry after every application.

Star: Use flat brush and antique gold to paint all sides of the wood star.

When dry, use black marker to add dashes to the front edges of star.

Gingerbread man: Use flat brush and toffee brown to paint all sides of gingerbread man.

Dip flat brush into black cherry and wipe excess paint onto paper towel. With a nearly dry brush, shade outer edges on front of gingerbread man.

Use liner and antique white to add wavy lines to ends of arms and legs.

Dip toothpick into black and dab on two tiny eyes.

Use black marker to add eyebrows and mouth.

Dip flat brush into red and wipe excess paint onto paper towel. With a nearly dry brush and a circular motion, add the cheeks.

Dip end of the paintbrush handle into black and dab three small dots down the front of the gingerbread man for the buttons.

Dip about 1 inch of remaining toothpick into burnt orange for snowman's nose.

Mug: Wash and dry mug.

Use liner and black to write "WILL WORK FOR COCOA AND COOKIES" on one side of mug. Let dry.

Dip end of paintbrush handle into black and add dots to ends of letters.

FINISHING: Use point of scissors to make a tiny hole in the snowman just below the eyes.

Break off painted end of toothpick. Glue painted end into hole for nose. Let dry.

Wrap fabric strip around snowman's neck and tie ends in an overhand knot. Glue star to knot. Let dry.

Put a bit of glue inside mug and add Spanish moss.

Glue pine garland pieces, berry stems and shovel inside the mug in back.

Glue snowman and gingerbread man inside mug in front. Let dry. ❄

Fig. 1

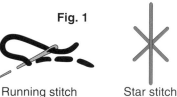

Running stitch   Star stitch

SNOWMAN
Trace 1—
tracing paper
Cut as
directed—
white
flannel

Trace, flop and repeat for complete pattern

Leave
open

Spread Cheer With a Charming Bookmark

A HAPPY ENDING is always in store when you use this pretty page-saver from Kathryn Pieters, of Burlington, Wisconsin. She embellished a purchased Aida cloth bookmark and added a fun charm accent. The cross-stitched piece makes a thoughtful gift for any book lover on your Christmas list.

MATERIALS NEEDED:
Chart on next page
7-1/2-inch x 2-1/2-inch 18-count white Aida cloth bookmark (Kathryn used one by Charles Craft)
DMC six-strand embroidery floss in colors listed on color key
Size 24 tapestry needle
7-1/2-inch x 2-1/2-inch rectangle of white fabric
10-inch length of 1/8-inch blue satin ribbon
10-inch length of narrow silver cord
Small silver snowflake charm
Paper-backed fusible web
Scissors

FINISHED SIZE: Excluding ribbon and cord, bookmark measures 7-1/2 inches high x 2-1/2 inches wide. Design area is 127 stitches high x 41 stitches wide.

DIRECTIONS:
Refer to the photo at left as a guide while creating bookmark as directed in the instructions that follow.

CROSS-STITCHING: To find the center of the Aida

cloth bookmark, fold the bookmark in half crosswise, then fold it in half lengthwise and mark where the folds intersect.

Draw lines across the chart, connecting opposite arrows. Mark where lines intersect. Begin stitching here for a centered design.

Each square on the chart represents one set of fabric threads surrounded by four holes. Each stitch is worked over one set of threads with the needle passing through the holes.

The color and/or symbol inside each square on the chart, along with the color key, indicates which color of six-strand embroidery floss to use to make cross-stitches. Wide lines on the chart show where to make backstitches. See Fig. 1 below for stitch illustrations.

Use 18-inch lengths of six-strand embroidery floss. Longer strands tend to tangle and fray. Separate the strands of floss and thread needle with two strands for all cross-stitches. Use one strand for all backstitches.

To begin stitching, leave a 1-inch tail of floss on back of work and hold tail in place while working the first few stitches over it. To end stitching, run the needle under a few stitches in back before clipping the floss close to work.

FINISHING: Lay the stitched bookmark vertically in front of you with wrong side up. Hold the ribbon and cord pieces together with ends even and center them vertically on back of bookmark, positioning them about 5/8 inch from the right-hand edge of bookmark and leaving ribbon and cord ends extending beyond top and bottom of bookmark.

Following paper-backed fusible web manufacturer's instructions, use paper-backed fusible web to adhere the ribbon and cord pieces to the back of bookmark.

In same way, use paper-backed fusible web to adhere the 7-1/2-inch x 2-1/2-inch piece of white fabric to the back of bookmark with edges even.

Tie the silver snowflake charm onto the cord end at top of bookmark. ❄

Fig. 1

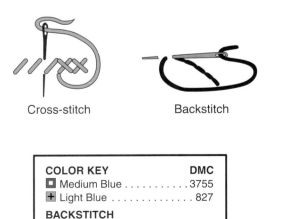

Cross-stitch   Backstitch

COLOR KEY   **DMC**
▢ Medium Blue 3755
✚ Light Blue 827
BACKSTITCH
— Silver E415

BOOKMARK CHART

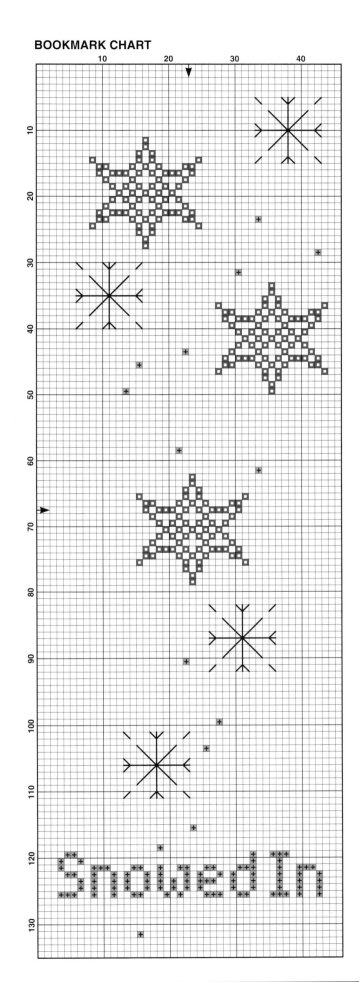

Take a Shine to Felt Candle Mats

YOU'LL BRIGHTEN the season even more when you make these folksy table toppers from Loretta Mateik, of Petaluma, California. She created three delightful designs—poinsettias, Christmas trees and gingerbread men—to go underneath jar candles.

MATERIALS NEEDED:

(For all):
Patterns on page 108
Straight pins
Tracing paper
Pencil
Compass
Scissors
Embroidery needle
Beading needle

(For poinsettia mat):
36-inch-wide wool felt—1/3 yard of white and 1/8 yard of red
Six-strand embroidery floss—red, green and gold
Seed beads—green and yellow

(For tree mat):
36-inch-wide wool felt—1/3 yard each of red and white

Scraps of wool felt—green and dark brown
Six-strand embroidery floss—green, white and black
Sead beads—red, white and yellow

(For gingerbread man mat):
36-inch-wide wool felt—1/2 yard of green
Scraps of light brown wool felt
Six-strand embroidery floss—white, dark brown and black
Black seed beads

FINISHED SIZE: Each felt candle mat design is 12 inches in diameter.

DIRECTIONS:
Refer to the photos above and at far right as a guide while creating the felt candle mats as directed in the instructions that follow.

Use beading needle when sewing beads and use embroidery needle for all other stitching.

POINSETTIA MAT: Use compass and pencil to make a 12-inch circle pattern on tracing paper. Trace poinsettia pattern separately onto tracing paper with pencil. Cut out patterns.

From white felt, cut two 12-inch circles. From red felt, cut eight poinsettias.

Place one poinsettia on one white circle about 1/2 inch from the edge, then place another poinsettia on top of first poinsettia so that the top petals are positioned between the bottom petals. In same way, position three more poinsettia stacks evenly spaced around circle. Pin all in place.

Using two strands of red floss, blanket-stitch around the outer edge of each top poinsettia piece only. See Fig. 1 on page 108 for stitch illustration.

Using one strand of gold floss, pick up one green bead followed by one yellow bead. Pass the threaded needle back through the green bead only. Stitch the bead set to the center of one poinsettia.

In same way, sew seven more sets of beads around the center bead set to form a circle.

In same way, add beads to each remaining poinsettia.

Pin remaining white circle to back of decorated white circle with edges even. Using two strands of green floss, blanket-stitch around the edge of both circles to join them.

TREE MAT: Use compass and pencil to make a 12-inch circle pattern on tracing paper. Trace tree, trunk and enlarged snow ring patterns separately onto tracing paper with pencil. Cut out patterns.

From red felt, cut two 12-inch circles. From white felt, cut one snow ring. From green felt, cut four trees. From dark brown felt, cut four trunks.

Center snow ring on one red circle. Position four trees and trunks evenly spaced along inside edge of snow ring, overlapping the trunk ends with the snow ring and tree bottoms. Pin all in place.

Using two strands of white floss, blanket-stitch around the outer edge of the snow ring.

In same way, sew a running stitch around inner edge of snow ring. See Fig. 2 for stitch illustration.

Using two strands of green floss, blanket-stitch around outer edge of green section of trees.

Using one strand of black floss, sew yellow, white and red seed beads to trees for ornaments.

Using two strands of white floss, stitch snowflakes on the red center area of decorated red circle. See Fig. 3 for stitch illustration.

Pin remaining red circle to back of decorated red circle with edges even. Using two strands of white floss, sew a running stitch around the edge of both circles to join them.

GINGERBREAD MEN MAT: Use compass and pencil to make a 12-inch circle pattern on tracing paper. Trace gingerbread man pattern separately onto tracing paper with pencil. Cut out patterns.

From green felt, cut two 12-inch circles. From light brown felt, cut four gingerbread men.

Position four gingerbread men evenly spaced around one green circle about 1/2 inch from the edge. Pin all in place.

Using two strands of dark brown floss, blanket-stitch around the outer edge of each gingerbread man. See Fig. 1 for stitch illustration.

Using one strand of black floss, sew black seed beads for eyes, nose and buttons on each gingerbread man.

Using one strand of black floss, make single stitches for each of the eyebrows and a "V" shaped stitch for the mouth on each gingerbread man.

Using two strands of white floss, make a running stitch to resemble zigzag lines of icing on the arms and legs of each gingerbread man.

Pin remaining green circle to back of decorated green circle with edges even. Using two strands of white floss, blanket-stitch around the edge of both circles to join them. ❇

(Patterns on next page)

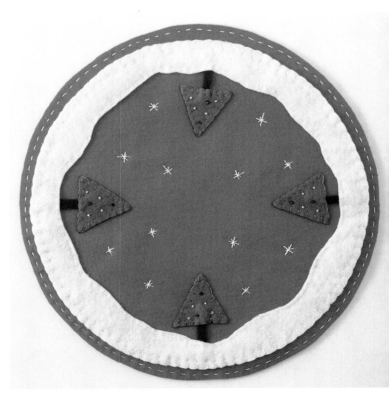

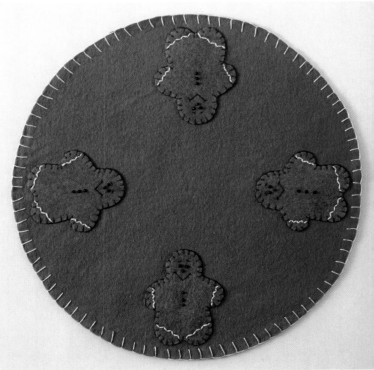

CANDLE MAT PATTERNS
Enlarge Snow Ring pattern 200%
Trace 1 each—tracing paper

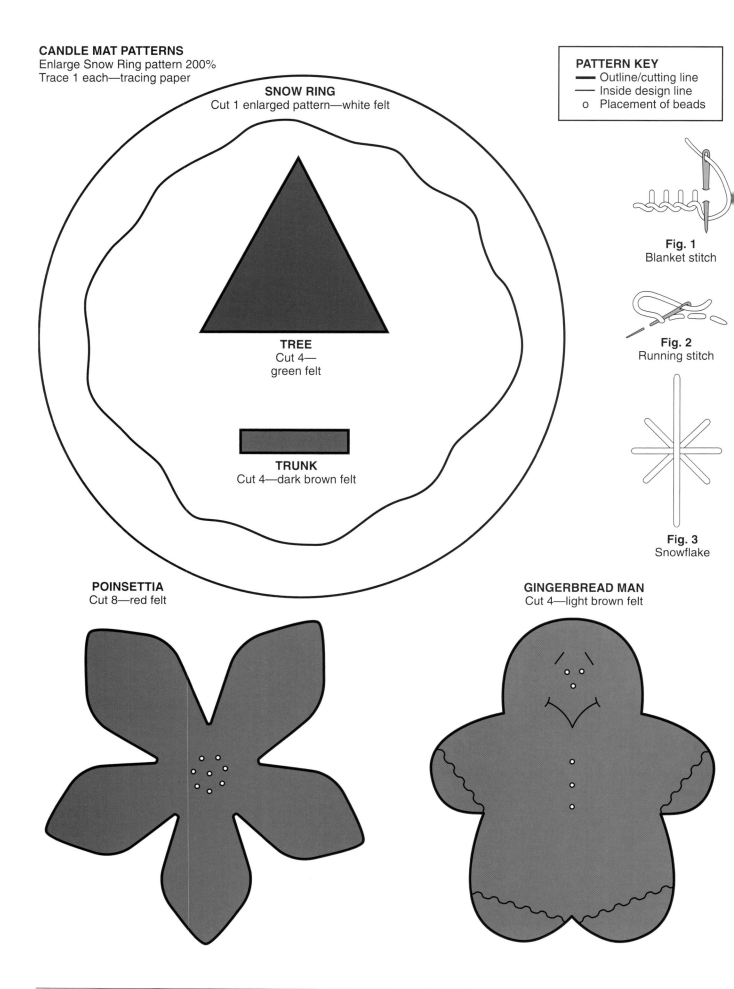

SNOW RING
Cut 1 enlarged pattern—white felt

TREE
Cut 4—
green felt

TRUNK
Cut 4—dark brown felt

POINSETTIA
Cut 8—red felt

GINGERBREAD MAN
Cut 4—light brown felt

PATTERN KEY
━━ Outline/cutting line
── Inside design line
o Placement of beads

Fig. 1
Blanket stitch

Fig. 2
Running stitch

Fig. 3
Snowflake

Scrapbook Page Has Sweet Memories

TREAT YOURSELF to this fun photo idea from CW Associate Editor Amy Glander. She created a festive page that's perfect for preserving snapshots of holiday cooking and baking. You could make all sorts of fun variations, too—for example, add tabs for journaling or a list of the Christmas treats you made.

MATERIALS NEEDED:

Patterned paper (Amy used Doodlebug Design Christmas Candy collection)—12-inch square sheet each of pink dessert-themed paper and polka-dot paper

Card stock—12-inch square sheet each of white, lime green and pink

Scalloped-edge polka-dot sticker strip (Amy used Doodlebug Design)

Rickrack sticker strips—one each of brown, pink and lime green

Round corner punch

Desired letter stickers—pink and lime green

Paper punches—2-inch scalloped oval, 2-inch circle and 2-1/2-inch circle

Assorted stickers (Amy used Doodlebug Design)—gingerbread house, gingerbread man, Christmas tree and cookie platter

Self-adhesive rhinestones—light pink, dark pink and green

Dark pink sheer ribbon

Scrapbook adhesive

Dimensional adhesive

Ruler

Scissors

Paper trimmer (optional)

FINISHED SIZE: Scrapbook page is 12 inches square.

DIRECTIONS:

Refer to the photo above right as a guide while assembling the scrapbook page as directed in the instructions that follow. Use scrapbook adhesive for all gluing unless the instructions say otherwise.

Cut a 10-inch square from pink patterned paper. Glue to center of 12-inch square of white card stock.

Cut an 8-inch x 7-1/4-inch rectangle from polka-dot paper. Glue to center of pink patterned paper.

Trim scalloped-edge sticker strip to a 12-inch length. Adhere to page bottom so sticker strip is overhanging the page edge slightly.

Trim green rickrack sticker strip to 12 inches and adhere to the top of page. Adhere the remaining two strips so they crisscross near the bottom of page, then trim strips even with the page edges.

Trim three photos to desired sizes and round the edges with corner punch. For photo mats, cut three pieces of green card stock that are slightly larger than each of the photos. Round the edges with corner punch. Glue photos to corresponding-size mats and set aside.

Cut a 2-3/4-inch x 3-3/4-inch rectangle from green card stock and cut a 2-1/2-inch x 3-1/2-inch rectangle from pink card stock. Round edges of both pieces with corner punch. Lay pieces vertically in front of you, then glue the pink piece to the green piece so that the top edges are matching and the pink piece is centered horizontally.

Using oval punch, cut an oval from polka-dot paper. Attach rhinestones to oval. Cut a 1-1/2-inch piece of ribbon, fold into a V shape and glue center of ribbon to top back of oval. Glue embellished oval to top of pink card stock piece and adhere house sticker to bottom of piece. Glue entire embellished pink-and-green piece to upper left corner of page.

Glue the matted photos as desired onto the center area of page, leaving space for remaining embellishments to be added to page.

Adhere pink letter stickers to spell "Sweets" on bottom right corner of pink patterned paper. Adhere green letter stickers to spell "Christmas" on photo above "Sweets."

Adhere the gingerbread man sticker to the top right corner of the page and adhere the Christmas tree sticker to the bottom left corner of page. Adhere a green rhinestone to the top of tree.

Using 2-1/2-inch circle punch, cut a circle from white card stock. Using 2-inch circle punch, cut a circle from pink card stock. Adhere the cookie platter sticker centered on the pink circle. Using dimensional adhesive, glue the pink circle centered on the white circle. Glue entire circle embellishment over the intersection of the crisscrossed rickrack strips at bottom of page.

With 2-inch circle punch, cut two circles from polka-dot paper. Cut each in half. Arrange three half circles evenly along the right edge of pink patterned paper on page, lining up the straight edges of half circles with the edge of pink patterned paper. Glue in place.

Let scrapbook page dry completely. ❄

A Christmas I'll Never Forget...

✳ *Special Feature* ✳

Charitable Cheer

Like most families, we celebrated the Christmas holiday by exchanging purchased gifts. Not long ago, we decided to try something new—and it started with skipping gifts for each other completely.

Instead, everyone chipped in the money we would have spent on presents. After contacting a local social service agency, we learned of a less-fortunate family in our area. Then we went shopping with our combined money to buy them much-needed clothing and food.

For the finale to our out-of-the-ordinary celebration, my oldest daughter cooked up a nontraditional main course of "Christmas chili" featuring red and green peppers. With finger foods, it made a wonderful holiday dinner.

We all agreed it was our best December 25th ever.

—*Wanda Rogers, Galena, Missouri*

Too Much Excitement

My sister-in-law and I were shopping together when she noticed some Christmas "poppers." She told me about her mother's tradition of including these paper noisemakers on their holiday table.

Inspired, I later bought some as a surprise. When I popped one at the table during my sister-in-law's Christmas feast, I anticipated everyone's delight. I'd placed a popper at each plate so the whole crowd could join in the fun.

They never got the chance. A visiting family's large dog, lying under a small table topped with food, panicked at my "pop." He yelped and jumped straight up, sending bowls flying. Gravy, dressing and cranberry sauce all landed on my sister-in-law's beautiful white carpet.

She was very gracious about the mess, and we enjoyed the rest of our celebration without further incident. But to this day, Christmas poppers make me cringe!

—*Julie Polderdyke, Sarasota, Florida*

Thanks for the Ride

When our sons were 10 and 6 years old, they both dreamed of getting a snowmobile. My husband and I knew they would be thrilled to receive one and would have a lot of fun riding it. But we had to tell them quite frankly that we couldn't afford such an expensive item.

Two weeks before Christmas, we returned home in the evening to find our answering machine blinking. Listening to the message, we were astonished to hear a voice stating we had won a raffle that had been held at the county fair. The prize? A new snowmobile!

I'll never forget how our sons' faces lit up in amazement and wonder at this unforeseen, dream-come-true gift.

—*Brenda Knable, Bagley, Minnesota*

Twice-Baked Treats

Making dozens of cookies is a Christmas tradition of mine. So is hiding them from my husband, who will gobble them up at any opportunity.

One year, I put plastic containers full of cookies in the oven, figuring he'd never look in there. My ploy worked… until days later when I absent-mindedly turned the oven on. It didn't take long for the air to fill with the stench of burnt cookies and molten plastic!

Armed with pot holders, I tossed the whole hot, smelly mess outside and into a snowbank. When my husband came home, he spotted the melted globs lying in the snow, guessed what they were and burst into laughter.

—*Lauren Winger Cotton, New Wilmington, Pennsylvania*

Dashing Through the Snow

Just before Christmas, our mother discovered that our car's instrument panel wasn't working. Unable to read the gas gauge, speedometer or anything else, we assumed we'd be homebound for the holidays and would have to cancel our plans to visit relatives.

On Christmas morning, without much hope, we went out to the car and turned the key in the ignition to see what would happen. To our amazement, the dashboard lit up and the meters worked! We decided to take the chance of going on our holiday rounds…and ended up going everywhere we wanted to with no car problems at all.

A few days later, the instrument panel went out again. But we weren't too annoyed. Instead, we were grateful it had worked on the most special day of the year. And we're convinced our guardian angel moonlights as a mechanic!

—*Leigh Ann Kesler, Rantoul, Illinois*

Music to Her Ears

As a teenager, I developed a passion for music and loved playing the bassoon in the high school band. My parents saw how much I enjoyed it and wanted nothing more than to buy me a bassoon of my own.

But purchasing a $1,000 instrument was no easy feat, considering the meager income Dad earned as a farmer. I had accepted the fact that having my own instrument was probably not going to happen.

On Christmas morning of my junior year in high school, my parents told me to look under the sofa for my present. Discovering a long, black case, I burst into tears. I knew instantly what it was—and realized the financial sacrifice my parents had made for me.

That bassoon accompanied me to college. I went on to teach music and play my Christmas gift in an orchestra.

—*Sara Studebaker, Loveland, Ohio*

Recipe and Craft Index

Stocking pattern below is for the Stocking Cake recipe on page 71. Enlarge pattern 200%.